That Your Joy Might be Full

By
Joseph Luke Palotta, M.D.

REVELATION HOUSE
PUBLISHERS, INC., METAIRIE, LOUISIANA

ISBN 0-9604852-1-X

Published By
Revelation House Publishers, Inc.
Post Office Box 73175
Metairie, Louisiana 70033

Manufactured In The United States Of America

To My Wife, Martha Lee,
For Introducing Me To Jesus Christ By
Demonstrating His Character,
For Her Courage And Faith In What He Would
Do With My Life,
For Loving Me, Michelle, Micah, and Christen;

And

To Her Parents, Earle And Ruth Cefalu, For
Giving Me A Christian Wife Through Whom God
Worked To Make This Book And Much More
Possible.

Table Of Contents

Acknowledgements

All Scripture references not otherwise indicated are from the King James Version of the Bible.

Scripture references from the Good News Bible - Old Testament: Copyright © American Bible Society 1976; New Testament: Copyright © American Bible Society 1966, 1971, 1976 - are used by permission.

Scripture references from the Revised Standard Version of the Bible - copyrighted 1946, 1952, © 1971, 1973 - are used by permission from the National Council of the Churches of Christ In The U.S.A.

Scripture reference from the Modern Language Bible, The New Berkeley Version, In Modern English, Copyright © 1969, © 1973 by Zondervan Publishing House, is used by permission.

Scripture reference from The Jerusalem Bible, copyright © 1966 by Darton, Longman, & Todd, Ltd. and Doubleday And Company, Inc. is used by permission from Doubleday And Company, Inc.

Probability estimates in Chapter One on the fulfillment of Old Testament prophecies are taken from **Science Speaks,** by Peter W. Stoner and Robert C. Newman, copyright 1968 by Moody Press, Moody Bible Institute of Chicago, and are used by permission.

The Faith, Prayer, and Tract League granted permission to quote from their tract No. 202, **Is This Success?** This tract is available from their ministry at Grand Rapids, Michigan, 49504.

Mrs. Shirley LeBlanc faithfully and patiently typed the manuscript.

Introduction

The preaching of Jesus Christ can be divided into two major subjects: how to get to heaven, and how to experience a good life on this earth. He preached on the kingdom of heaven, but much more of his preaching was on how to enter the kingdom of God in this life. The kingdom of God is characterized by the conditions of peace, joy, and fruitfulness. One is inevitably either in this kingdom of God, or in a state of despair.

In the Gospel of John 15:10-12, Christ preaches, *"If ye keep my commandments, ye shall abide in my love; even as I have kept my father's commandments, and abide in his love. 11 - These things have I spoken unto you, that my joy might remain in you, and that your joy might be full. 12 - This is my commandment, that ye love one another, as I have loved you."* Here is one of the least recognized and least understood facts of Christianity. Christ both promises and instructs that if we follow His commandments, not only will we experience joy, but our joy will be full.

This promise of joy for following the teachings of Christ recurs throughout the Bible. At the beginning of the First Epistle of John, 1:3-4, the apostle writes and promises, *"That which we have seen and heard declare we unto you, that ye also may have fellowship with us: and truly our fellowship is with the Father, and with his Son Jesus Christ. 4 - And these things write we unto you, that your joy may be full."*

Long before I became a Christian, I discovered that those psychological techniques which successfully eliminated anxiety, fear, and depression, were merely re-statements of the teachings of Christ. Each day that I have practiced psychiatry since becoming a Christian, it has become ever more obvious to me that Christ's teachings provide the most effective methods of obtaining mental health that one can find.

Throughout this book, it is demonstrated how scriptural instructions for relating to God, others, and oneself, will produce peace and emotional health. I thus present these reflections on applying the Scriptures to life today, "that your joy might be full."

Section One:
Successful Christian
Relationship
With God

1

The Observable Validity Of Christianity In Life Today

A tract entitled, **Is This Success?**³ describes a group of the world's most successful financiers who met at the Edgewater Beach Hotel in Chicago in 1923.

"Collectively, these tycoons controlled more wealth than there was in the United States Treasury, and for years newspapers and magazines printed their success stories and urged young people to follow their examples. Here is the rest of the story:

"1 - Charles Schwab - the president of the largest independent steel company - lived on borrowed money the last five years of his life, and died penniless.

"2 - Richard Whitney - the president of the New York Stock Exchange - served time in Sing Sing.

"3 - Albert Fall - the member of the President's Cabinet - was pardoned from prison so he could die at home.

"4 - Jesse Livermore - the greatest bear in Wall Street - committed suicide.

"5 - Leon Fraser - the president of the Bank of International Settlement - committed suicide.

"6 - Ivar Krueger - the head of the world's greatest monopoly - committed suicide.

"More modern examples of business men, movie stars, and sports figures could be added to the list. All of these people learned how to make a fine living, but not one of them had learned how to live. Have you?"

The Faith, Prayer, And Tract League, which publishes this tract, informed me that they have verified the truthfulness of these statements according to the records of these six men in The Chicago Tribune. This type of data certainly suggests that some of these men may not have given adequate attention to the spiritual dimensions of their lives. The outcome was tragic.

In February of 1978, Time Magazine[7] published a story about Saudi Arabian Princess Marshall bint Abdul Aziz, and her lover, who were both executed by the government for allegedly conducting an adulterous affair with each other. An uproar of international protests resulted. Reports from Saudi Arabia indicated that the couple had been dealt with more leniently than usual. Under Saudi religious law, the penalty for adultery is public stoning to death. It was interesting to me that these people were utilizing Old Testament Law.

Later on, I found another article in one of the medical journals about Saudi Arabia. The Saudi Government was upgrading that nation's medical care facilities, and they were trying to recruit American doctors to Saudi Arabia to staff the multi-million dollar medical facilities which they were building. They badly needed members of every medical specialty but one. They did not need any psychiatrists. That article went on to say that the reason they had no need for psychiatrists was that most of the population followed the Islam religion very closely. They maintained their family units and their extended family ties. They consequently relied on their religion and on their family relationships whenever they were in any kind of crisis. People seemed to have very reliable roles that they felt they should fulfill. They consquently seemed to function with more stability than we are accustomed to seeing in the United States during times of personal or family crisis.

The Islam religion accepts the Old Testament, and its members worship Jehovah. They do not accept Christ as the Messiah. Instead, they regard Him as a prophet. Though their religion is thus very different in important ways from Christianity, they are having a relationship with the same God.

Some time after seeing these articles, and prior to the overthrow of the Shah, I met a physician from Iran, another Islam country. This doctor had practiced medicine in the United States for several years. I asked whether he had any experience that would confirm or deny any correlation between the mental health of the population of Iran and their religious beliefs. He replied that he had practiced medicine in two very different areas of Iran. One area was in the Capital City of Tehran, a large westernized metropolitan area. In this area, he described the Iranians as being "liberated" from their Islam religion. They were culturally very similar to the populations of large cities in the United States. He had found that psychiatrists in Tehran were quite overworked. Psychiatric hospital facilities there were overpopulated with too many patients for the number of available psychiatrists. The same spectrum of anxiety, depression, psychomatic and psychotic problems seen in U.S. medical practice were seen in Tehran.

Another area in which the Iranian physician had practiced was a large, rural area approximately one hundred fifty miles from Tehran. The population in this sparsely populated area adhered closely to its Islam religion. There he would mainly perform what may be called triage: determining who needed to go to the hospital in the capital city, or who could do without that, and rendering what medical care he could at the moment. He said that he was responsible for 150,000 people in that population. This large number is indicative of the great scarcity of medical care in that part of that country. He had the opportunity to see firsthand what the general health of the population was really like. He had found that most of the patients he saw in that rural area had medical problems which were genuine, organic problems. There was little if any of the chronic anxiety, depression, and psychosomatic symptoms that are so common in the experiences of doctors in Tehran or in the United States.

There seems to be a close correlation between one's relationship with God, or the lack of it, and one's emotional health.

The Theory Of Evolution Is Falling
Into Progressive Disrepute

The theory of evolution has caused many to doubt the validity of the Bible and the existence of God. Several aspects of the theory of evolution have come under attack by science itself. One of those controversial areas involves the work of many anthropologists who dig up human skeletons. The heavy vocational pressure on those men to continue getting financial grants through their universities, and to continue getting advancement in their departments of anthropology creates a heavy pressure upon them to continually make "new" discoveries. Whenever they unearth a skeleton, there is little if any attempt to correlate that skeleton with all of the other finds that have been made in that area or other areas. The emphasis is to try to place **their** names on that skeleton, saying, "This is an original find. This is a different man from anything else that has been discovered before. This is a new man." Also, there is a tendency to dig up a small portion of bone and then to reconstruct the original appearance of an entire person from it. Anthropologists themselves have begun criticizing many of their colleagues for doing this. The criticism that comes from the anthropologists is that this is not science: this is imagination. It is simply not scientifically possible to dig up a small piece of bone, and from that to reconstruct the appearance of an entire person. Yet, this very thing is done frequently. It makes good cover stories and feature articles for magazines. It no doubt helps the anthropologists to advance in their careers, but it is not really valid.

14

Another important objection to the theory of evolution comes from science itself. The second law of thermodynamics may be summarized as follows. With the passage of time, systems change spontaneously in the following ways: from orderly to disorderly, from complex to simple, and from high potential energy to low potential energy. The theory of evolution obviously violates all aspects of these basic principles of science. Scientific objections to the theory of evolution are reviewed in the book, **In Six Days,** by C. H. McGowen, M.D.[5]

Skeletons have been unearthed which anthropologists claim are millions of years old. It is generally thought that the Bible does not go back that far. The fact is that we do not really know how far back in time Genesis goes. That information has simply not been given to us. At times in the past, theologists such as Bishop Usher have thought that they could date the events in Genesis, but they were subsequently discovered to be in error. There is an interesting theological theory that might account for some of these skeletons that are thought to be quite old. Genesis 1:1-2 (King James Version) tells us, *"In the beginning God created the heaven and the earth. 2 - And the earth was without form, and void; and darkness was upon the face of the deep. And the Spirit of God moved upon the face of the waters."* Here we have a picture of the earth being quite void. However, in Isaiah, Chapter 45, Verse 18 (Good News Bible), we are seeing a picture of a very different earth. *"The Lord created the heavens — he is the one who is God! He formed and made the earth — he made it firm and lasting. He did not make it a desolate waste, but a place for people to live. It is he who says, 'I am the Lord, and there is no other God.' "* These would initially seem to be two contrasting pictures of the earth as its creation. Many theologians feel that a large era in time occurred between the first and second verses of Genesis Chapter One. They assert that God originally created the earth in a form on which man could live as Isaiah describes. They theorize further that the earth was initially populated by people who lived under the rule of Lucifer, prior to his rebellion against God. This theory holds that at the time that Lucifer and those who followed him rebelled, the earth was then destroyed and made void. God subsequently re-created the earth, and it is this re-creation that the rest of the Book of Genesis really describes. Noted theologians such as W. A. Criswell[1] and F. J. Dake[2] adhere to this theory for which there is some Scriptural basis.

The theory of God's creation of earth, its destruction and recreation gains some additional evidence from Genesis 1:27 and 28 (King James version): *"So God created man in his own image, in the image of God created he him; male and female created he them. 28 - And God blessed them, and God said unto them, Be fruitful, and multiply, and replenish the earth. . . ."*

According to this version, Adam and Eve were instructed to **replenish** the earth, implying that it had once been filled with people and wiped out. The original Greek word used here can be interpreted as either "fill" or "replenish." We consequently have evidence for this theory rather than proof. Nonetheless, when you add all that up, there is certainly no reason whatsoever to discredit the Scriptures because of any anthropological finds. As a matter of fact, the history of archaeology very well supports the Bible, and never discredits the Scriptures. Though there have been long periods of time in archaeological history when some archaeologists felt that they had caught the Bible in a mistake, later finds always proved that they were in error, and that the Bible was correct.

Personal Evidence of God's Existence

My personal life has led me to realize the validity of Christianity through experience. During childhood, I attend a Catholic church and catechism. I was brought up as a Catholic. At eighteen years of age, I began studying philosophy in college, and discovered that all of the doctorates of philosophy in that department were atheists.

They preached atheism, and I did not know anything about the Bible other than the brief excerpts from the Gospels which had been presented in the middle of the Latin masses I had attended. Those philosophers were intellectually impressive, so I figured that they were probably right. For the next fourteen years, I did not believe that God was real. I read Darwin's books on evolution, and the works of "modern" philosophers who denounced God's existence. But in the back of my mind, I realized that there was a potential error in the atheistic position of the "modern" philosophers. They had defined God the way that **they** wanted to define Him. They created an abstract, logical system, and had defined God out of that abstract system. I knew that even though that sounded good on a blackboard, it did not define God out of external reality. I knew that I needed more information about that subject, because it was so very important.

Over the ensuing years, I studied medicine, then psychiatry, and then began practicing psychiatry. I discovered that trying to live life only by means of intellect and psychological knowledge without a relationship with God frankly messed up my personal life. I came to the inevitable conclusion that I could not direct my own life with my own will alone, even in spite of having become a well-trained, successful psychiatrist. When I looked at the high suicide rate, the depression, and all of the other personal problems among psychiatrists, I realized that my colleagues did not seem to be doing very well in their personal lives either. It appeared to me that something more was needed. At about age thirty-two, as I continued to accumulate information, I began to realize that everything that I knew was really beginning to look quite consistent with the existence of God. Only by acknowledging God's existence could I explain what I had seen and learned of life and of the world.

I then began to notice some important patterns in my work. I had been exposed to all sorts of psychological theories. Some of them seemed to be very sound, some were of questionable value, and some of them were worthless or even harmful. I gradually accumulated a large repertoire of things which I said to people in emotional difficulty that would effectively turn their lives around, away from despair, away from anxiety, away from fear, away from depression, and toward joyful, peaceful life experiences. I began to realize that all of those things which I had been doing and recommending that had turned lives around toward health were identical to the teachings of Christ. Everything that I had said or done in the effective practice of psychotherapy was something that Christ had taught. Nothing that I was doing, or had done, that had ever really made a difference in a person's life, was in any way contrary to what Christ had taught. I said to myself, "Isn't that interesting? Wasn't Christ a good phychologist? Wasn't He smart? I haven't caught Him in a mistake yet!" I gradually accumulated enough information to realize that nothing that I knew contradicted the validity of Christ, His teachings, His principles, or the Bible. At that time, I made a decision to become a Christian.

Some time afterwards, I began to notice something even more interesting in my work. Everyone who was coming to me for emotional problems also seemed to have at least one spiritual problem. At the time their problems had begun, there was always something that they had been doing which had been somehow different from the ways Christ taught that we should handle our thoughts, feelings, words, or actions. I could always identify something in the life of every troubled person which was somehow a violation of something that Christ had taught. That seemed striking to me, because I was not accustomed to seeing anything present 100% of the time. This is not what doctors usually see. An illness may be successfully treated by one medicine in a certain percentage of people. Another percentage of people with the same illness will not be helped by the same medication. Yet another percentage of people with the same illness may die or experience bad reactions in response to the same medicine. This is the variety of human experiences that physicians are accustomed to seeing in their daily experiences. Though one usually does not see things happening 100% of the time in any kind of medical or human experience, I continued to see this 100% factor. Some violation of one or more of Christ's teachings had always begun the emotional trouble. I was initially mystified by this. It sounded like something Christ would do, but I did not understand it. During the same period, I was reading the Bible for the first time since I had become a Christian. I came to a passage that I had seen and heard many times. That was Luke, Chapter 6, Verses 46-49: *"46 - And why call ye me, Lord, Lord, and do not the things which I say? 47 - Whosoever cometh to me, and heareth my sayings, and doeth them, I will shew you to whom he is like: 48 - He is like a man which built an house, and digged deep, and laid the foundation on a rock: and when the flood arose, the stream beat vehemently upon that house, and could not shake it: for it was founded upon a rock. 49 - But he that heareth, and doeth not, is like a man that without a foundation built an house upon the earth; against which the stream did beat vehemently, and immediately it fell; and the ruin of that house was great."*

It suddenly dawned on me that this section of Luke was really a set of promises. Christ is promising a life of strength and peace for following His teachings, and a broken life of despair for rejecting His instructions for living. I then realized that the entire Bible is constructed around promises exactly like these, in different words, but with the same meaning. Over and over, we are promised peace, joy, fruitfulness, and a sound mind for living by what Christ taught, versus despair for rejecting Him and His instructions for living.

Romans Chapter 1, Verse 28, tells us: *"And even as they did not like to retain God in their knowledge, God gave them over to a reprobate mind, to do those things which are not convenient."*

I then realized that if I were not seeing the things that I had been seeing, if I had not been observing the 100% factor, that somebody would have been making a liar of Christ. If ever I were to witness somebody who had been violating Christ's teachings and had found peace, and joy, and fruitfulness, that person would be making a liar of God. Likewise, if ever I were to see someone who was following all of Christ's teachings and who thereby experienced despair, depression, anxiety, or an inability to function normally, he would be making a liar of the Lord. That has simply never occurred. I began to realize that the promises in the Scriptures could be observed throughout the experiences of the people who had come to see me for their problems. It became strikingly apparent to me that all of life is affected by the promises of God.

Life Experiences Today Prove That God Never Breaks His Promises

These scriptural promises were illustrated by the life of a middle-aged man who was having an awful problem with an illness that is referred to as manic depressive psychosis. Technically, no one knows the cause of this emotional disorder, though there are many theories about it. This man had become suicidal and had to be admitted to a hospital. This had occurred many times before in his life, for the same problem. He was feeling as if he were at the end of his rope. I told him that there was something strange happening in what he and I had done to address his illness. I had treated him for some time, and we had used medications in attempting to control his illness. I had been taught in my psychiatric training that this type of illness did not respond very well to psychotherapy, and that one really had to use medications as the primary method of controlling it. I had used every medicine that was likely to have any chance of helping him. Each time that his mania or depression recurred, a new medication was tried, and he would have a dramatic response

20

for several weeks or several months. Then he would suddenly enter a depression or mania again in spite of having continued to take his medication on a maintenance basis. At this point, I said, "Look. The Lord is not letting us have a lasting healing for you. There is something that we are missing, or overlooking, that he wants changed. We need to find what it is, so that this thing can get straightened out, because I cannot see any other reason that you would be having this experience."

With his consent, we then conducted a rapid analysis of his manic-depressive episodes. Concentrating upon his problem, he began to review the past regarding the causes of his trouble. He began recalling a series of very, very painful childhood rejections from his father. He re-experienced the despair that he had felt as a small boy, when he wanted so much to have his father's affection. Instead, he was continually rejected, to the point that he finally developed a kind of on-going, chronic bitterness toward the father. He then proceeded to say, "You know, I realize that this is also the cause of the alcoholism that I suffered from years ago. All of those drunken episodes were gigantic tantrums, because I was angry at my father, even then. I would go out and get drunk and carry on, doing anything that I felt like doing, hurting anybody that I wanted to hurt. Then I got to the point where I created so many severe problems that I could not continue that. I just ended up in this present illness as a substitute." I said to him, "Now that you realize that all of this trouble is coming from all this bitterness toward your father, why don't you just forgive him and release yourself from all that bitterness? Then you won't have to go through this awful experience anymore." He replied, "I just can't do that, Doc. Can't do that." I said, "What do you mean, you can't do that? Why not?" He then said, "Well, I feel that if I forgive my Daddy, he's going to get away with what he did."

I asked, "Do you believe in God?" He said, "Yes." "Do you believe in the Bible?" "Yes." I said, "Do you realize that the Bible says that no sin will go unpunished?" "Yes."

"God has already given you a written guarantee that He has taken care of your father's behavior. You don't have to do it in this manner." He said, "No, Doc. That's not true. My Daddy is dead, and he never got punished for that." I said, "Well, I don't know what happened that you could say that, but I know that God does not work that way. I have seen enough of life to know that nobody can do the kind of things that you described on the part of your father, and go unpunished. That's just not the way life is. I would like for you to think this over, because there is something wrong in what you tell me. Something is missing here. I will come back tomorrow, and see you again. There has got to be a resolution to this thing."

When I returned the next day, he said, "You know, after you left, I realized that the last several years of my father's life, he was crazy. He was psychotic and senile. He constantly thought that people were after him to retaliate for something that he had done, and he didn't know what it was. He could never figure out what it was. He was continually looking over his shoulder, looking behind himself and wondering when someone was going to get him. This was the kind of tormented experience that he had. I didn't want to remember that, because I am afraid that the same thing is going to happen to me!"

Here you can get a glimpse of the absolute reliability of God to keep His promises in life today. You can count on His promises to that extent that if someone contradicts them, you can reliably say, "Hey! I know that you are wrong. Now let's figure out where it is you went wrong in your thinking." I did that here. I did not hesitate to stake my professional reputation on this promise which God has repeated in both Testaments, to let no sin go unpunished. God was right, and this man had been wrong. This is the kind of experience that I have over and over again, in talking with people and in looking over their lives with them. This man made a decision that he was going to partially forgive his father, and he received a partial cure. Several years have passed without his being manic or suicidally depressed, though he has experienced a mild, chronic depression. This was far better than he had gotten before, but it really was not as much as he could have received. It was not total health. It was not total stability. It was not the peace and the joy, or the kind of fruitfulness that Christ promises. This man understood what the problem was. He understood what he must do about it. That was all that he was willing to receive of what Christ was willing to give to him.

Life Experiences Prove That Jesus Christ Is The Same Today As In Biblical Times

A young woman had a long history of recurrent medical illnesses that had caused many hospitalizations. It seemed as if she could never be really healthy. As soon as one problem seemed to be resolved, some other serious health problem would occur. She told me that whenever she had to give her history to a new doctor, it would depress the doctor to hear that so many awful things had happened to one person. Naturally, she was depressed and in despair. She was also having spiritual problems, wondering, "Is God really there? Why would He let all of this happen to me?" After she told me all that she could, and I asked her all the questions that I could, we still did not understand why she was having all of this trouble. I said to her, "You know, your life reminds me of Job. He went through the kind of experience that you are going through now. Perhaps it is a different nature of illness from his. Nonetheless, the way you are feeling today is the way Job felt. The Bible says that Jesus Christ is the same yesterday, today, and forever. He's got to be the same today as when he inspired those Scriptures. When we look through the Book of Job, we see that there were some things in Job's life that God wanted to change before He would restore Job's health." I shared with her that the Book of Job, 3:25-26 tells us, *"For the thing which I greatly feared is come upon me, and that which I was afraid of is come unto me. 26 - I was not*

23

in safety, neither had I rest, neither was I quiet; yet trouble came."

The Bible makes it clear that before Job's tribulation began, there was fear in his heart. He was not at peace, no doubt as a result of that fear. He could not feel safe, or at rest, or quiet. He had felt troubled even before real trouble came. God did not want that fear to exist in Job's heart. In the dialogue between Satan and God at the beginning of this Book, Satan told God that if ever Job got into a very bad situation, that Job would curse God. God must have seen something in Job that caused Him to agree with Satan, because He let Satan proceed to test Job's faith. As this test of faith unfolded, Job lost his wealth, his children, and then his health. When Job's health was affected, Job did, in fact, begin to curse the day of his birth. In essence, Job then questioned the Lord. He took the position that God was wrong to let all of this happen to him. Furthermore, if God would just let Job have an audience with Him, Job felt that he could show God how unfair He was being to Job. As this continued, I suppose that God must have realized that Job was not going to learn what he should be learning and building in his character from these experiences. God consequently gave Job a personal audience. When Job saw the majesty of God, he realized that God could not be wrong! He realized then that somehow, whatever God was doing in his life was right. When Job realized that spiritual truth about God and about his relationship with God, his health was restored.

I explained to this woman that these events took place in Job's life thousands of years ago, because there were some things in Job's life that God wanted to change. I asked her, "I wonder if these health problems are God's way of saying, 'Hey! There is something that has got to be changed in your life for your own benefit before your health can be restored!' I wonder what it could be?" She said, "You know, I just figured out what it is! Sometime ago, I received an invitation to commit adultery with a guy, and I never said 'No' to him. I

24

just left it open, so that I could always go through that door anytime that I wished. I have just been chronically tossing it over in my mind, whether I was going to do that or not. I realize that that is why I am here today. I have just been torturing myself, using any possible excuse to punish myself because of what I have been considering and leaving myself open to do."

Another truth in the Scriptures is revealed by this woman's experience. In Matthew 5:28, Christ preaches, "But I say unto you, That whosoever looketh on a woman to lust after her hath committed adultery with her already in his heart." This suggests that if a person yearns for adultery, he begins to feel and act as though he had already committed it. That is what was happening to this woman. She had yearned for this experience, and was acting as if she were an adulteress who had to be punished. Anytime she encountered any ache, pain, or illness that looked like it could be the punishment that she deserved, she would nurse it, make it grow, and milk it for every bit of suffering that she could obtain from it. Through self pity and self punishment, she was taking small physical problems and mushrooming them until she became depressed. The depression was then causing all sorts of other physical changes in her body that were wrecking her health. One can easily see the validity of the Scriptures in this person's life.

Life Experiences Demonstrate That God Keeps His Promises To Answer Prayers Of Faith

A successful businessman sought help for alcoholism, depression, and marital problems. A series of awful experiences with alcohol had wrecked his family. When I spoke with him about his spiritual life, he told me that he was agnostic. He had serious doubts about whether God was real. I could see that awful damage was taking place in his life as a result of his being spiritually lost. The lack of any **spiritual** understanding or stability was causing **emotional** instability

25

in his life. For some reason, of all the things that I could have told this man, I said, "You know, there are many promises in the Bible, and you can see the validity of those promises today. They are just as reliable now as they were in the days they were written. I think that it would mean a lot to you to familiarize yourself with some of these promises, to see what is in the Bible and how it may pertain to your life today." He knew very little about the Bible. He replied, "Speaking of the Bible, the other day I was drunk in a bar. I had been there for several days. I had torn up my family so badly, that my wife would not let me come back home for fear of what damage I might do to the children or to her. For some reason, I felt an irresistable impulse to go to my mother's house. So I got out of the bar, and I went to my mother's house at 3:00 p.m. that day. Well, I later learned that at that time, my mother and my wife had begun praying together that I would leave that bar and go to my mother's house. My wife was afraid of having me in our home in the drunken condition that I was in, and yet she did not want me to stay in the bar. Those two had begun praying, and there I went! It is extremely unusual for me to go to my mother's house in the middle of the afternoon." Then I told him about the promise in Matthew 18:19-20 where Christ said, *"Again I say unto you, That if two of you shall agree on earth as touching any thing that they shall ask, it shall be done for them of my Father which is in heaven. 20 - For where two or three are gathered together in my name, there am I in the midst of them."* They were asking for something which was certainly consistent with what Christ would want them to ask, that a person he delivered from a drunken binge. We could see those promises of Christ being kept in this man's life today.

The Fulfillment Of Bible Prophecy Proves
The Validity Of Christ And The Bible

In addition to all of the other means of validating Christ and the Bible, it can also be done by means of Bible prophecy. Peter Stoner and Robert C. Newman wrote a book entitled, **Science Speaks.**[6] These men presented the mathematical probabilities of certain Old Testament prophecies being fulfilled if they had been made on the basis of mere **human** prediction. Old Testament prophecies predict the futures of several of the ancient cities around the Mediterranean sea. The ancient city of Tyre, located on the eastern coast of the Mediterranean, was inhabitated by the Phoenicians, who gave us part of our alphabet. The Old Testament Book of Ezekiel, in Chapter 26, contains seven prophecies which Ezekiel uttered in approximately 600 B.C., regarding the future of Tyre. All seven of those actually took place. The city was ultimately destroyed in the exact manner that the Bible predicted. Peter Stoner and Robert Newman determined that the mathematical probability that all seven of those predictions in Ezekiel would befall any one city is one in seventy-five million. Yet all seven events happened to the city of Tyre!

Jeremiah, in approximately 600 B.C., prophesied that Jerusalem would one day be enlarged. In the Book of Jeremiah, 31:38-40, he precisely described the new boundaries to which the city would be enlarged. The chance of all of these exact, detailed prophecies taken as a conglomerate being fulfilled is one chance in eighty billion! Nonetheless, every one of them took place exactly the way Jeremiah prophesied.

The Books of Leviticus (26:31-33) and Ezekiel (36:33-35) contain seven prophecies about Palestine which were all fulfilled. Those prophecies in Leviticus were estimated to be made between 1400 and 1520 B.C. The prophecies in the Book of Ezekiel are estimated to have been made between 592 and 570 B.C. The probability of all seven of these prophecies taking place together was calculated to be one chance in twenty thousand. Yet, they were all fulfilled.

Isaiah (13:19-22, 14:23) and Jeremiah (51:26, 43) uttered a total of eight prophecies about the City of Babylon. The probablity of all of those things happening to any one city was calculated to be one in five billion! Yet, all of these have occurred in the subsequent history of Babylon. One can thus see the tremendous odds against mere human prediction having been involved in the utterances of Biblical prophecies.

The life of Christ fulfilled sixty-one Old Testament prophecies about his personal life. Stoner and Newman took only eight of those prophecies and calculated the probability that any one human life could accidentally fulfill all eight of them simultaneously. The probability of that happening turned out to be one chance in 1×10^{17}. In ordinary language, that turns out to be one chance in a hundred thousand trillion that one ordinary human life would fulfill even eight of the sixty-one Old Testament prophecies that Christ's life fulfilled. Some people say, "Well, maybe Christ just fulfilled those things on purpose. He was an expert on the Old Testament. He knew what prophecies were." The reply to that would have to be that many of the fulfilled prophecies about the life of Christ were things totally beyond anyone's ability to control: such as the Messiah's place of birth, His time of birth, the circumstances of His birth, that He would be betrayed by a friend, the manner of His death, that people would mock Him, that His body would be pierced, that there would be no broken bones in His body at death, and that he would be buried in a rich man's tomb.

The subject of Bible prophecy and the historical evidence for Christianity is covered quite thoroughly in Josh McDowell's book, **Evidence That Demands A Verdict.**[4] That book is an anthology (summary) of a large number of books on apologetics (defense of the faith). I highly recommend a reading of that work.

I have only presented an extremely small portion of the available evidence for the validity of Jesus Christ. The evidence is overwhelming that He was exactly who and what He said He was. Even on the basis of such a small amount of the available evidence as I have presented here, one would have to conclude that anybody who would reject Christ would have to be very uninformed, very foolish, or both.

Bibliography

1. Criswell, W.A. **The Scarlet Thread Through The Bible.** Nashville: Broadman Press, 1970.
2. Dake, F.J. **Dake's Annotated Reference Bible.** Lawrenceville, Georgia: Dake Bible Sales, Inc., 1963.
3. Faith, Prayer, And Tract League. **Is This Success?** Grand Rapids, Michigan. This ministry makes this publication available as Tract No. 202. It is quoted here by permission.
4. McDowell, Josh. **Evidence That Demands A Verdict: Historical Evidences For The Christian Faith.** Revised Edition. San Bernadino, California: Here's Life Publishers, Inc., 1979.
5. McGowan, C.H. **In Six Days.** Van Nuys, California: Bible Voice, Inc., 1976.
6. Stoner, Peter W. and Newman, Robert C. **Science Speaks.** Chicago: Moody Press, Moody Bible Institute. Copyright 1968. The authors' probability estimates of the fulfillment of Old Testament prophecies are used by permission.
7. **Tragic Princess.** Time, 111:46, Feb. 13, 1978.

2

Solutions To Spiritual Problems
Seen In Psychiatric Practice

Sigmund Freud was so heavily addicted to cigars that he smoked twenty cigars a day. At age thirty-eight, he began making repeated attempts to stop smoking, but was never able to do it. Whenever he would discontinue the cigars, he would enter such a horrible depression· and intolerable withdrawal symptoms, that he would resume smoking. In 1923, he developed cancer of the mouth and jaw at age sixty-seven. Over the next 16 years, he had 33 operations for this condition. That was an average of more than two operations a year for cancer. He had to have the entire jaw removed and replaced with a jaw prosthesis. At times, he was in constant pain, and could not speak, chew, or swallow; but he continued smoking cigars. Finally, in 1939, at age eighty-three, after a forty-five year unsuccessful struggle to stop smoking, he died of his cancer.

Freud did a great deal to advance psychological theory, and though a great deal of what he wrote was helpful, some of it was erroneous. In **The Future Of An Illusion,**[1] Freud asserted that a belief in God is merely a neurotic, illusory attempt to maintain one's dependent childhood relationships with parents. Here one can get a tiny glimpse of the price that Freud probably paid because of the lack of spiritual depth in his life. It appears that he was having serious problems directing his life, and that he lacked some important answers to living that all of his psychoanalytic theory did not provide.

Freud's primary answer to life seemed to be that all one needs to do is to make the subconscious conscious, and that will solve all of his problems. His own personal life appears to have been a poor testimony for that theory.

Modern psychiatry traditionaly pays little or no attention to the spiritual aspects of human problems. Most psychiatrists seem to be agnostic, and even embarassed to engage in any thought or discussion of the idea of God, or to address the spiritual dimension of emotional disorders. This is the apparent result of Sigmund Freud's atheistic influence. Psychiatrists often make the common error of assuming that because Freud developed a large number of valid psychological theories and concepts, it is safe to assume that **everything** that he wrote was true. Yet, even Freud's psychoanalytic theories have come under progressive attack by modern psychiatry. The psychiatric profession pays a high price for this shallow orientation to life and its problems. Psychiatrists demonstrate a suicide rate that is several times that of the general population, as well as a high incidence of depression and divorce.

The reputation of modern psychiatry suffers because of its reputation for a lack of concern with spiritual matters. People who are in need of psychiatric treatment often delay obtaining it for years. Many fear that psychiatric treatment does not help people. They have often heard of others who obtained psychiatric help which was terribly expensive, slow in its results, or of no help at all. This attitude is quite prevalent. Many emotionally ill people wait until they cannot live with their emotional problems anymore before obtaining help, because they have had such pessimistic attitudes about the ability of psychiatry to help them.

I would like to share with you some of the experiences that I have had, looking at small segments of the lives of people with severe emotional symptoms that were basically caused by spiritual problems. Each of these people was essentially incapacitated and could no longer live very productively.

They could not fulfill their personal or family obligations, and many of them could no longer fulfill their vocational obligations. Many of them were very suicidal. The underlying spiritual conflict in each of these cases was diagnosed, and instructions were given for proper resolution of the conflict. This was followed by an almost immediate elimination of their emotional symptoms. People often do not receive healing in psychiatric consultation because (1) the cause of the problem is really a spiritual one, (2) the spiritual aspect of the emotional problem never gets diagnosed, (3) since it is not diagnosed, it is never addressed, and in some cases, (4) even if it **were** diagnosed, the therapist is not prepared to deal with such problems as a result of his agnosticism and lack of familiarity with the Bible.

Acknowledging That God Fulfills His Own Responsibilities Produces Healing

The first of these situations that I want to mention is that of a young woman who was in an explosion. This woman was essentially unharmed by the explosion, but her sister was severly burned in the same explosion. Her sister had to be hospitalized for several months, and had a very painful recovery. The woman who was uninjured developed a severe depression, insomnia, and was unable to remember things very well anymore. She was having severe difficulty in her job because of her inability to concentrate. The evaluation revealed that much of this symptom complex was being caused by guilt that her sister had been so badly hurt, while she was essentially unharmed. This is referred to as **survivor guilt**.

Her survivor guilt was healed in one session. The answer that she needed was given when it was pointed out to her that she was subconsciously assuming God's responsibility for what had happened. She had been giving no thought to the fact that God could have prevented that explosion, that He could have killed both of them in the explosion, that He could have caused her to be as badly injured as her sister. She was a Christian, and was asked to consider the following concepts. God would not let something like this happen without reason. He would most likely provide what He knew was needed in her life, and in the life of her sister. It was probable that her sister needed something to get built in her emotional and spiritual life that would not have been built without that experience. Whatever that something was, the uninjured woman already had those character strengths, and did not need that experience.

I had previously consulted with the woman's sister, and I knew that this very thing had happened. When the sister had gotten burned, her personality seemed to totally fall apart. I have consulted with many people who were burned as badly or worse than she had been. Her emotional response to her situation was far worse than one usually sees in such cases. Her response was to immediately regress to the emotional level of a helpless child who was hurt, angry, and in a bitter tantrum. She demanded that others do everything for her, and would do nothing to help herself mentally or emotionally. Her personality looked even worse than did her burned body. She had absolutely no emotional or spiritual preparedness with which to deal with stress. The outcome of her ordeal was impressive. At the time she was ready for discharge from the hospital, I asked her, "Has any good come out of this for you? Has anything gotten built in your life as a result of this?" I wanted to know what God was doing with this woman's life. She said, "Yes. I am a much more mature individual. I feel that I could handle things now that I could never have faced before my accident." As a result of her experience and the psychiatric consultation she received for the emotional complications of her burns, she learned to reject the feelings of total helplessness that were a basic part of her old self image.

It took only approximately five minutes to explain to the uninjured sister that she merely needed to consider that God knew what He was doing. The events of the explosion and her sister's injuries were not her responsibility, but God's. Her survivor guilt was immediately cured, and it did not take months or years of therapy to accomplish this.

Acknowledging That God Appoints A Time To Die Produces Healing

A middle-aged man had to be hospitalized in a psychiatric facility because he was severely depressed, suicidal, and could not stop drinking alcohol. He had no idea why he was so depressed, though he was in such despair that he wanted to end his life. A rapid analysis of his depression was conducted. When he was asked to review the past regarding causes of it, he recalled that decades before, he had escaped from a foreign country during a revolution. He had such a narrow, miraculous escape that it was difficult for him to imagine how he escaped alive. In spite of the incredible odds against his survival, he escaped and was able to establish a life in this country. He had killed a member of the local political regime in that country during the course of his escape to prevent being killed by that individual.

The reason that he was so depressed was that he had lived in continual expectation that spies from that country would hunt him down to execute him in retaliation, as they had promised to do. Here he was, decades later, still waiting to get killed, wondering when it was going to happen. It was pointed out to him that if God had wanted him to die, he could have been very easily killed decades ago during the escape effort. As a matter of fact, the hardest thing to understand was how he **had** escaped. He had escaped under heavy fire, had even been shot, and was carried over the border by a friend. He was urged to consider that God would determine the length of his lifespan and appoint the time of his death (Ecclesiastes 3:2). It was really not up to the enemy agents. That had already been dramatically demonstrated. If somebody were to try to take his life, he would take whatever measures that he could to prevent it; but the outcome would be up to the Lord, as it had been before. That healed his depression. Within two more days, he was discharged from the hospital and resumed his job. He was healed by the realization that God maintains sovereignty over his life as well as over the time of his death. I have seen many people receive healings of their fear and despair the moment that they saw and accepted this spiritual truth.

Recognizing God's Love Produces Healing

A man in middle life was suffering from a number of emotional problems, including chronic alcoholism. He just could not stay away from liquor. He had a tendency to become depressed, and the alcohol would physically depress him further. A slight depression would thus become severe despair once he started drinking. He would then experience the problems of drunkenness, inappropriate social behavior, and marital problems. His wife objected to his drinking, and would "get on his case," so to speak, whenever he drank. He would then feel rebellious and resentful about her nagging. The drinking was thus causing some problems, and complicating other problems.

A rapid analysis of his drinking problem revealed that during his adolescence, he made his Catholic Confirmation. He had experienced a great lack of fathering in his childhood. During the Confirmation service, he began to feel a real spiritual high. He felt very close to the Lord, and had never felt so good in his whole life. After the Confirmation ceremony, he and some of his buddies had a party to celebrate. There was wine there, and he started drinking. The thought then entered his mind that he felt so great that it must be the wine that was making him feel so good. He then began to think that if he stopped drinking the wine, he would lose this great feeling: so he kept drinking, and drinking, and drinking, and got terribly drunk. From age twelve, when he was confirmed, to middle age when I treated him, he had spent many decades trying to reproduce that spiritual communion with God by means of alcohol. It did not work. It never had. But he thought that it would.

When the past was reviewed, he recalled very clearly that the spiritual high that he experienced at age twelve really took place in the church, before he had drunk even a drop of alcohol. He realized that it was not the alcohol which had made him so happy.

That one session healed that man's alcoholism. I have a five year follow-up, and he has not had a problem with liquor since then. Alcoholism is a very difficult problem to cure. As a matter of fact, the only permanent healings that I have ever seen of that disorder have been through spiritual considerations in which an improvement in the individual's relationship with the Lord was an important part of the cure. Even though psychological matters often must be addressed, the spiritual dimensions of it must be addressed if the healing is to last.

Claiming God's Promises Of
Protection Produces Healing

A young widow sought help for a severe depression, a phobia of being alone at night, and insomnia as a result of the fear of being alone. Her husband had died a few years before. With the passage of time since her husband's death, her fear, insomnia, and depression were increasing. She was doing poorly, and had no idea why she was so afraid. When some thought was given to her fear and how it got started, she realized that she felt a great deal of dependence on her husband. She had a young child, and felt that being alone at night with no man in the house to protect her, made her very vulnerable to burglars, or to anyone who would wish to come in. She felt quite helpless, and as if she had no protection at all. This problem had caused this woman a long period of emotional turmoil, to the point of incapacitation and the loss of her mental health.

She believed in God and believed that the Bible was God's

word, but she did not know much about it. She was asked to consider the following concepts. In many places in the Scriptures, God promises to be the special protector of widows and fatherless children.[2] While she had, in fact, lost the protection of her husband, she had gained the protection of God in an extraordinary way. She had entered a very special category of people in God's eyes. Rather than having her husband to protect her, she now had those written guarantees of God's protection. She could place herself under that protection with far greater certainty of protection than she had before. The presentation of these simple, but important Biblical concepts eliminated all of her emotional symptoms!

Trust In God Produces Healing

A man who sought help for a previously incurable smoking problem was heavily involved in Christian work. He had substantial seminary training, but was a liberal theologian. He did not believe that one could trust the Bible as the literal Word of God. He was also becoming subtly but progressively addicted to alcohol and to barbiturate headache tablets. Every evening cocktails were used to relieve tension. He had even traveled to several cities in search of a healing of his smoking addiction. Everything had failed, including psychoanalysis, and behavioral modification. Nothing had worked. So far as I could tell, the main thing that did finally produce his cure was a consideration of the spiritual aspects of his problem. He experienced a great distrust of God the Father, because during his early childhood, God had taken his earthly father in death. He felt the way most children do who are not properly instructed at the time of a father's death. He felt that God had taken something from him that he vitally needed, and without which he could not survive. Consequently, there was no telling what God was going to do next. In his subconscious he wondered, "How could I place my trust in the Lord?" Rather than place his trust in God, he

37

was placing his trust in tobacco and other addicting chemicals. He led a relatively stressful life because of the magnitude and responsibilities of his vocational position. When he was under stress, he would rely on cigarettes, barbiturates, and alcohol, because these were tangible. He could see them, and he felt that he could control them.

The emotional aspects of his addition had been thoroughly analyzed. His difficulties seemed to boil down to this one spiritual problem that was behind everything else. He was urged to consider that the primary problem was not emotional, but spiritual. He felt that that was correct; but I could tell that he had gotten angry, because I did not have seminary training, and he did. I could tell that he did not like for me to talk with him about theology, and he was sensitive about it. I knew that I would make him angry if I brought up his spiritual problem, but I also knew that this was the only answer to his difficulties at that point. He had already tried every possible form of treatment for his problems, and he had defeated every one of them.

As I suspected, he dropped out of treatment after I shared my understanding of the spiritual problem behind his addictions. Approximately a year later, I accidentally saw him in public and I asked him how things were going. He told me that several months after that last session with me, he had finally kicked the smoking, the alcohol, and the barbiturates! It appeared that this spiritual insight was the main thing that produced the healing.

Accepting God's Provisions Produces Healing

A middle aged woman complained of severe anxiety, depression, and insomnia. All of these symptoms had begun when she and her husband, who had always maintained a low middle class economic status, experienced a very profitable reversal of their financial life. They had just purchased an expensive house on a prestigious street in their community.

The interview revealed that she was in this emotional distress because she felt the Bible teaches that we are supposed to be meek, and there did not seem to be anything meek about living in a very expensive house. She was referring to one of the Beatitudes in Matthew 5:5, *"Blessed are the meek: for they shall inherit the earth."* It was pointed out to her that the concept of meekness that Christ taught there probably referred primarily to one's relationship with the Lord. We are to be meek toward God. This meekness consists of the realization that whatever God wants to provide for us is the best thing for us, based on His love and wisdom for our lives. This is not saying that we are supposed to purposefully maintain a low status in our relationships with our fellow men. Abraham, Isaac, and Jacob were apparently wealthy men according to the Bible's description of their lives. David was not exactly meek in his relationship with Goliath, whom he slew, but he **was** meek toward the Lord. David gave God the credit for what was going to happen or did happen in his life. King Solomon, of course, was not poor either.

It was also brought to her attention that God often uses money as a means of teaching people important lessons which build emotional, spiritual, and character strengths. A person whose financial circumstances force him to live on a very small amount of money often has experiences which build compassion, ability to cooperate more successfully with other family members in addressing their problems, and thriftier use of God's provisions to him. A poor person who suddenly gains a great deal of money may then have the opportunity to build character by learning to use his assets to **help** others rather than to harm them. He often has opportunities to learn new and higher levels of social, vocational, and financial functioning. A wealthy or middle class person who suddenly **loses** his fortune may learn to rely more heavily upon his relationship with God than when he relied mainly upon money for security. He may then become familiar with the absolute faithfulness and reliability of God.

It took only one session to discuss these concepts. A month

later, her next session revealed that all of her anxiety, depression, and insomnia had been eliminated in response to those considerations. The outcome of her new financial situation was that her husband now felt confident to entertain prominent business, professional, and political leaders in their home. She gained new confidence and self-respect by functioning as a successful hostess of these gatherings. This was a higher level of interpersonal or social function than she had ever before experienced, and it was brought about through God's financial blessings upon her!

Recognizing God's Wisdom And Faithfulness To Keep His Word In Our Lives Produces Healing

A suicidally depressed man felt like killing his mother as well as himself. He had lost all incentive to work or to support his wife and children. These symptoms had suddenly begun several days before, when he had made a telephone call to his chronically psychotic mother who lived in another state. He told her that he realized that the main thing wrong with his life was that he had never experienced a close relationship with her. He felt that he should establish such a relationship with her now. Her response was that she did not want anything to do with him! She did not even know him. She had been in asylums all the while he was growing up. In spite of the large family depending upon his support, he had felt so overcome with rage that he had not worked since that transaction had occurred.

Several things were presented to him that reversed the entire problem in half an hour. This man was a Christian who was quite familiar with the Bible, which he accepted as God's word. It was pointed out to him that the Scriptures promise that no sin goes unpunished (Numbers 14:17-18, Matthew 26:52, Revelation 14:10). When he reviewed his mother's life and saw how much time she had spent in asylums, there was no question that she had been adequately punished for

40

anything that she had done wrong to him. There was thus no need for his holding grudges to try to punish her, or retaliate. This man was also urged to consider that God had obviously been protecting him by removing that hostile, deranged mother from his life during the critical, formative years of his personality development. Even though he had been brought up in an orphanage that he had not liked very much, it had been a much better psychological atmosphere than the one to which he would have been subjected had he been confined in a house with a woman who was apparently as mean as she was insane. His father had been a weak man who permitted his son to enter an orphanage rather than to fulfill his own parental responsibilities.

He was urged to consider what God was trying to build in his life by those particular childhood experiences, including losing that mother and being brought up in an orphanage, as well as some of the tribulations that he had experienced in the orphanage.

He responded that there was no question in his mind that a tremendous compassion for other people had been built in his life as a result of those experiences. He could really tell how other people were feeling, and he would never treat his children, or anyone else the way his parents had treated him. Even though he had ended up in an orphanage, he felt that he was now a much better human being in many important ways as a result. He felt immediately healed of his depression, his wish to commit suicide, his wish to kill his mother, and his inability to work. I saw him and his wife in consultation two years later, for a separate problem that was being caused by the wife, and which had nothing to do with his former difficulties. He had experienced no recurrence of any of these problems.

I am always amazed by the incredible healing power of recognizing that God will do exactly what He has promised, while revealing His love for us and providing the best things for our lives. I once presented this case in a talk in a seminary. One of the students voiced concern that God would punish every sin, and punish this man's mother.* It must be considered that God was also reaching out to his mother. She was apparently saying "No" to God, and "Yes" to those extremely bitter feelings which produce psychoses. God uses tribulation and the punishment for sin to try to turn our lives away from despair and toward peace. Unfortunately, stubborn self will often blinds us to God's revelation of Himself and the good life that He wants to give us. We merely need to recognize and accept the wisdom of His instructions and provisions, which are based on His love for us.

A woman was experiencing a long list of emotional problems, including chronic depression and extreme obesity as a result of feeding that depression. An interview revealed that an important cause of both the depression and the obesity was a great deal of bitterness towards her father, because he had rejected her from birth. She knew certain things about this man, but she had never even seen him, nor had he ever looked for her.

She was asked, "What happened to that father?" The answer was that when she was five years old, this fellow was pursuing his chronic narcotic addiction. Apparently under the influence of narcotics, he went to bed smoking a cigarette, fell asleep, and burned himself to death. She was then asked, "What would have happened to you if that father had not been removed from your life?" The obvious answer was that she would have been burned up with him! She was then urged to consider God's promises to protect the fatherless,² which had in fact been kept. Her childhood environment had been quite disorganized due to severe character and emotional problems on her mother's part. Her mother's character and parenting had not been much better than her father's had been. This patient had never expected to survive childhood. Yet, she did. Her physical needs had

---

*A thorough analysis of this theological problem is given in the essay, **The Fatherhood of God In Life Today,** presented in Chapter Three.

always been met. She had a pleasant personality and a nice appearance, even in spite of her obesity. She now had a family, with children. Her main problem was that she had been so bitter about what God had permitted to happen to her during childhood, that she had never considered that those events had been designed for her protection as well as because of the character that God was trying to build in her. She felt that she was now a far better mother than she would have been without her personal childhood experiences with bad parenting.

Recognizing And Accepting God's Grace Produces Healing

A man sought help for a suicidal depression. His main wish was to die. He had never been able to relate to his children, and had been relatively unable to relate to his wife. His depression was robbing him of the joy that should have been a part of his life. When the cause of his depression was explored, it came to light that during his childhood, some incestuous behavior had occurred between him and a sister. He felt that he was going to hell for that, because God would never forgive him. He had a very rejecting, unforgiving earthly father, and he had been subconsciously expecting God to react to him in the same way. He expected that God would never forgive him, because he had never experienced a father's forgiveness in his earthly life.

Pointing out to him that his perception of God was identical to his perception of his earthly father rapidly reversed his entire set of emotional problems. The wish to suicide was gone, the depression lifted, he became able to relate very well to his children as well as to his wife, and he began a much more successful relationship with God.

An agnostic psychiatrist referred a man to me because of the failure of his rather extensive therapy with this patient, including a psychiatric hospitalization. The patient was overwhelmed with fear that he was going to die. He continually worried about whether anything was wrong with

43

his breathing and with his heartbeat. Physicians had checked him and rechecked him, and had assured him that he was physically well, but their assurances did not help his fear at all.

My immediate reaction to that history was to tell him, "If you are afraid to die, you have a **spiritual** problem." I then asked whether he believed in God. "Yes." "Do you believe in the Bible as God's word?" "Yes." Even though he was illiterate, he did accept the Bible as God's word. He did not know anything about it, however.

The interview revealed that this man had previously engaged in an extramarital affair which had been terminated several years previously. He believed that he was going to hell for that affair. I asked if he had confessed that sin to God. As a matter of fact, he had. Then he said, "I do not believe that God forgave me, though. I do not believe that God forgave me." I then read him the First Epistle of John 1:9, *"If we confess our sins, he is faithful and just to forgive us our sins, and to cleanse us from all unrighteousness."* I asked him why he had given up the affair. He said, "I just lost interest." I replied, "Isn't that interesting? The Bible promises here that if you confess your sins, you will be cleansed of unrighteousness, and that has already happened! Half of that promise of God to forgive and to cleanse you if you confess has obviously been kept. You have been cleansed of that unrighteousness. Now, all you need do is to place your faith in the other half of the promise, that *he is faithful and just to forgive us our sins."*

I also shared some Scriptures with him to the effect that God cannot lie or break a promise (Dt. 7:9, Nu. 23:19, 1 Sam. 15:29). He then rejected that erroneous belief, that lie, that God would never forgive him, and replaced it with the truth. The truth was that he was promised forgiveness. Forgiveness had already been given to him, but he had merely been refusing to receive it or to accept it.

I only saw that man for six sessions. Many months of previous therapy had been a total failure because neither the spiritual cause nor the spiritual solution of his illness had been recognized.

As you can see from these life experiences that I have shared with you, emotional distress is often caused by underlying, spiritual conflicts, and can be healed with spiritual truths. Spiritual problems are misunderstandings and misperceptions of one's relationship with God. It is very interesting to me that some 2000 years ago, when the Pharisee asked Christ (Matthew 22:36-40),

> *"36 - Master, which is the great commandment in the law?*
>
> *"37 - Jesus said unto him, Thou shalt love the Lord thy God with all thy heart, and with all thy soul, and with all thy mind.*
>
> *"38 - This is the first and great commandment.*
>
> *"39 - And the second is like unto it, Thou shalt love thy neighbour as thyself.*
>
> *"40 - On these two commandments hang all the law and the prophets."*

It appears that having a proper attitude toward God, others, and the self is also the basis for all mental health.

Bibliography

1. Freud, Sigmund. **The Future Of An Illusion,** trans. W.D. Robson-Scott, ed. James Strachey, Garden City, N.Y.: Anchor Books (Doubleday & Co., Inc.) 1961. The original German edition of this work was published in Vienna in 1927.
2. Scriptural references in which God promises that He will be the Father to the fatherless and the protector of widows:
   Exodus 22:22-24
   Deuteronomy 10:18; 14:28-29; 16:11, 14; 24:17-22; 26:12-13; 27:19
   Psalms 10:14; 10:17-18
   Psalms 27:10 *"When my father and mother forsake me, then the Lord will take me up."*
   Psalms 68:5; 82:3
   Proverbs 23:10-11
   Isaiah 1:17; 1:23-24; 10:1-2
   Jeremiah 5:28-29; 7:6-7; 22:3; 49:11
   Hoseah 14:3-5
   Malachi 3:5
   James 1:27

3

The Fatherhood of God
In Life Today

The Fatherhood of God is a unique and extremely important part of our daily lives. Many people make very erroneous assumptions about God's Fatherhood, and this alienates them from God.

A woman sought psychiatric help for a severe depression that had reached the point of despair. The depression had begun in response to a head injury which caused nerve damage to one ear. The nerve damage caused a continual roaring sound in this ear. The roaring was literally driving her crazy. She had been told by her ear, nose, and throat specialist that she would probably get well, but she wouldn't believe or accept that. Instead, she continued to worry continually. This worrying had caused her to become progressively depressed.

The theme of her worry seemed to be that she would never get well, and that she might have to spend the rest of her life with the roaring sound in her ear. She didn't know how she could ever stand that. She felt considerable bitterness toward God because He let this happen to her. This was causing a spiritual problem, an alienation from God, which resulted in further depression.

Interviews with her revealed that her self will was so exaggerated that it had become damaging to herself. If everything didn't go just the way that she wanted it to go, she felt as if some sort of disaster were occurring in her life. It was easy for me to see that this was most likely one thing that God was trying to change in her life, perhaps by means of this problem. It was also apparent that she had a pronounced tendency to engage in self pity and needless suffering in a mentally masochistic or self-damaging way. I shared these thoughts with her and began some psychotherapy aimed at these problems. She improved, but then dropped out of therapy before it was completed. Individuals who experience such a psychological tendency to hurt themselves sometimes quit treatment that would heal them, because of the subconscious wish to prolong the suffering and self pity.

I didn't see her again until nine months later. She had recently attended a large revival meeting. The minister, who had never seen her before, picked her out from the middle of the audience of several thousand people. The minister told the congregation that the Lord was telling him that a woman in her section of the auditorium had an ear problem that God wanted to heal. She didn't think that it could be she, so she didn't get up right away. He then described her clothing and appearance in such detail that she realized that he was speaking to her. At that point, she went to the front of the audience, where he prayed for her. She asked me what I thought that experience meant. Could it be right that the Lord did want to heal her? I told her that it seemed to me that this minister did have some kind of communication from the Lord, because she had no prior contact with him. He knew absolutely nothing about her, and had never seen her before. Yet he had picked her out of an audience of several thousand people and had identified this problem. This at least confirmed that he was receiving a most unusual source of information about her. I told her, "The Bible says that *Jesus Christ is the same yesterday, today, and forever* (Hebrews 13:8). He healed people yesterday. I don't see why he couldn't, or wouldn't heal you today, the same as He healed others 2,000 years ago."

She then obtained some of the therapy that I had

recommended nine months earlier. She responded with significant further improvement in her condition, both mentally and physically. This was remarkable in view of the fact that her ear specialist had recently told her that there was now no further hope of her getting any better, because of the length of time which had lapsed since the nerve damage had occurred. Yet, she did improve. Before she was fully healed, however, she again dropped out of treatment before completing all of the therapy which I had recommended. I don't know what her condition is today. I suspect that she is still experiencing some unnecessary suffering and illness that God really doesn't want her to have. She was simply not willing to receive or accept all that He was obviously willing to give to her.

This is just one example of what people go through as a result of feeling bitter toward God. Their lives would be much better were they to go to Him with faith in His love, His Fatherhood, His power, and His willingness to provide what they need. It's all too common that people simply say, "Well, God let this happen to me. He either doesn't love me or He doesn't have the knowledge and power to meet my needs." Phillipians 4:19 promises, "But my God shall supply all your need according to his riches in Glory by Christ Jesus." An observer can look at lives such as this one and see God trying to reach out to people. Because of their erroneous ideas of what God is like as a father, they reject Him as well as His provisions, and then become bitter about His supposedly rejecting them.

This type of spiritual problem is unfortunately common. I suppose that all of us have had similar spiritual struggles, are having them, or will have them, unless the nature of God's unique Fatherhood is properly understood.

Common Erroneous Assumptions About
The Fatherhood of God

It has been my experience that intellectual or emotional

errors are always present whenever individuals reject, doubt, or become embittered about God's Fatherhood in their lives. People often make intellectual errors. In talking with people about their spiritual lives, it is not unusual for someone to tell me, "The Bible contains a lot of contradictions. It contradicts itself." One reason that many feel that the Bible contradicts itself is that they have not read it from cover to cover with a spiritual understanding of the Holy Spirit. Such spiritual understanding comes from the faith that God is somehow always right, because He is infinitely wiser than we are. Without this orientation, one jumps to premature and erroneous conclusions about the reasons for God's actions.

It is common for the Bible to describe what God did in one book, and to say why he did it in a subsequent place in the same or other books.

Error: God Wrongfully Orders That People Be Killed

Throughout the Books of Moses and Joshua, God tells the Israelites to destroy every man, woman, and child in the land of Canaan (the promised land of Palestine). To the intellect, this sounds barbaric, because the reason for this judgment of God is not immediately stated. In subsequent O.T. books, such as Ezekiel 16:20 and Jeremiah 7:31, the Bible describes some of the awful forms of idolatrous worship that the Jews copied from the Canaanites, such as sacrificing their own children to heathen gods. In Exodus 34:15-16, the Bible records that God told Moses that if the Jews were to make any peace treaties with the people of Canaan, the children of the Canaanites would one day lead the children of the Jews into the same idolatrous practices. In Joshua 16:10, the Bible states that the Jews disobeyed God and permitted some of the Canaanites to survive and live among them. Subsequently, the Bible records that future generations of Jewish men committed whoredom with Canaanite women who led them into those idolatrous practices (Numbers 25:1-3, 31:16, Ezra 9:1-2, Revelation 2:14). The Jews subsequently became so

50

deeply entrenched in these heathen religious practices, that God found it necessary to provide long periods of Jewish enslavement at the hands of Assyrians, Babylonians and Persians for punishment: destruction of the Jews who were beyond reform, and refinement of those amenable to God's counsel and discipline. Only by getting all of this information can one begin to see that God's original instructions to the Jews regarding the Canaanites were all based on His perfect love, wisdom, and His wish to protect and provide for those who accepted Him as their Father.

Error: God Can't Possibly Love Us If He Punishes Every Sin

Another common intellectual error about the Fatherhood of God involves His punishment of sin. On one hand, the Bible says that God is all knowing, all powerful, and loves us so much as His children, that He was willing to sacrifice His own Son for us. He forgives us for our sins, and Christ submitted to crucifixion to make this possible. On the other hand, the Bible also teaches that this same God, our Father, permits the devil to afflict people at times. He lets no sin go unpunished. He enslaved his chosen people, the Jews, many times at the hands of cruel heathens for as much as 400 years at a time. He tells us that we must fear Him.

How can one reconcile these statements that at first glance might appear contradictory? How can we avoid this intellectual snare into which the average person seems to fall altogether too easily?

The answer to this is in the concept that is taught in the Book of Numbers, Chapter 23, Verse 9 (Good News Bible), *"God is not like men, who lie; He is not a human who changes his mind. Whatever he promises, he does; He speaks, and it is done."* God cannot lie, He cannot break a promise. He cannot do anything that can be identified as sin; and yet he loves us. For a moment, if you will mentally place yourself

51

in the position of one who can never lie, never break a promise, and never sin, you will realize that you would be one of the least free people in the universe. There would immediately be enormous numbers of things that you could never do! You would not be a free being, because you had bound yourself to be a totally ethical being. You would suddenly have to change many things that you might now do in your handling of everyday situations.

For example, if you had a child who broke one of the rules of ethics you had given him while you were a "normal" human, you would be free to **decide** whether you would punish him in some way. You would be free to give him another chance with the option not to punish him, unless he should repeat such behavior in the future; but if you were bound to be a perfectly ethical judge of your child at the same time that you were his father, such an option would not be available. You would be forced to administer some punishment for every wrongdoing, had you previously promised to do so.

We have a God who does love us, but He is simultaneously the perfectly ethical judge of the universe. It is like going before a court of law in which the judge happens to be your father. You may have committed a small crime or a large one. Visualize yourself in a court of law with your own father, who loves you, judging you. Visualize the eyes of the whole world on this judge, to see if he is going to be just with the son or daughter that he loves. Will he be corrupted by that love to be unjust, and unfair, by letting the son or daughter get away with the wrongdoing? This is the position in which God is. If any of us could be found to have really gotten away with sin, then God would have lied; He would have broken His promise to punish every sin. On the other hand, He really can't do that, you see. Just as the earthly judge would have to consider the effects of his judgment upon everyone else if his own son were in court, God must no doubt consider the effect that it would have if He were to let people get away with sin unpunished.

Error: How Can God Punish Me For My Sins, Since Christ Died For Them?

Christ shed His blood to free us from the ultimate effects of sin, and He promises to forgive us (1 John 1:9). Yet, He promises to let no sin go unpunished (Numb. 14:17-18, Mt. 26:52, Rev. 13:10). This results in a great deal of confusion and controversy among Christians. The apparent dilemma can be understood and resolved by the concept that when Christ died for our sins, He removed the ultimate penalty for sin, which is hell. Christ's atonement permitted God to modify the punishment for sin, so that He can select and apply punishment as a way of disciplining and refining us, building character in us, and as a way of revealing Himself to us. Throughout the Book of Ezekiel, Ezekiel prophesies all of the awful things that God is going to do to the Jews, if they continue their refusal to give up their child sacrifices (Ezekiel 16:20) and other idolatrous practices in which they were engaging. Each of these prophecies of God's future punishment concludes with the statement, *"And they shall know that I am the Lord"* (Ezekiel 6:10, 6:13-14, 7:9, 20:26, 24:24). The punishments of God are often so perfectly just, that individuals who receive them cannot escape the recognition of the perfect design of the punishment to match past sins. The Israelites rejected God to worship false idols and were subsequently enslaved by Egypt, where they were forbidden to worship God publicly. They engaged in child sacrifice, and during Nebuchadnezzar's seige of Jerusalem, starving Jews ate their own children. God thus uses punishments that are due for sin to refine us and to show His love by changing our lives. You can imagine what a dreadful person each one of us would become if we knew we could do anything that we wished and not have any consequences for it!

Genesis 18:23-26 (Good News Bible), offers a glimpse of the perfection of God's ethical judgment. *"Abraham approached the Lord and asked* (regarding Sodom), *'Are you really going to destroy the innocent with the guilty? 24 - If there are fifty innocent people in the city, will you destroy the whole city? Won't you spare it in order to save the fifty? 25 - Surely you won't kill the innocent with the guilty. That's impossible! You can't do that. If you did, the innocent would be punished along with the guilty. That is impossible. The judge of all the earth has to act justly.' 26 - The Lord answered, 'If I find fifty innocent people in Sodom, I will spare the whole city for their sake'.''* This dialogue continues to Verse 32 of this Chapter (Good News Bible): *"Abraham said, 'Please don't be angry, Lord, and I will speak only once more. What if only ten are found?' He said, 'I will not destroy it if there are ten'.''*

Theologians often express regret that Abraham stopped with ten men rather than proceeding to ask God if He would spare Sodom if only **one** good man were found in the city. The answer to this is found in Jeremiah 5:1 (Good News Bible). Here, Jeremiah has been prophesying the destruction of Jerusalem for its sinfulness. He says, "People of Jerusalem, run through your streets! Look around! See for yourselves! Search the market places! Can you find one person who does what is right and tries to be faithful to God? If you can, the Lord will forgive Jerusalem." Here the Bible is making it clear that even one good person seeking the will of the Lord and trying to follow it would have changed the history of Jerusalem! There can be no question about the absolute perfection of God's justice!

In Ezekiel Chapter 33, Verse 11, God makes it clear that He laments having to punish the wicked. But again, He has no choice: *"Say unto them, As I live, saith the Lord God, I have no pleasure in the death of the wicked; but that the wicked turn away from his way and live: turn ye, turn ye from your evil ways; for why will ye die, O house of Israel?''*

You can see the pain in the heart of the Lord in this prophetic message. God is asking Israel, "Why are you going to do all that evil and make it necessary for me to carry out what I know I will have to do if you continue all that?" This sounds like a father whose son has just engaged in such destructive behavior that it will probably be necessary for the son to go to prison or reform school: the father knows that if he doesn't let the child have the consequences of his rebellion, there will be no hope for him. Yet, it hurts the father. You can see this kind of anguish in this communication from God.

Error: There Is Something Wrong With God For Demanding Blood Sacrifice For Sin

What about the phenomenon of blood sacrifice? It is quite bothersome to many people that God has demanded the shedding of blood for the forgiveness of sins. They say, "Why is God so bloody? Do you mean to tell me that He wants the shedding of blood for sin? How can He do this and be everything else that He says He is?" Many seem to have trouble with this because they equate the shedding of the blood of Christ with the shedding of human blood. People seem to be mentally programmed so that the idea of bloodshed is always an awful or even a criminal thing. They begin thinking, "Well, if I were to shed my blood, it wouldn't do any good." They then mentally project this condition onto God and forget that when Christ shed his blood, this was **God's** blood that was shed. It wasn't an ordinary human's blood — it was God's blood. In some way that we don't understand, the shedding of God's blood did something that no human's bloodshed could do. People say, "Well, I don't understand that. I don't understand how Christ's shedding His blood is going to do people any good." They get caught in the intellectual snare of trying to understand this from the point of view of a human, and feel as if it is their responsibility to understand that. They overlook the concept that it is not **their** problem — this is God's problem. It is as if God were saying, "Look. People have sinned. Somehow, when I look at the blood of Christ, those sins have a different effect on me, and cause me to render different judgments. The penalty of sin has been modified and changed through the blood of my Son." The Scriptures make it clear that when God looks at Christ's blood, it means something special to Him that we can't understand: but we don't need to understand it. It's not for us, it's for God to understand. It satisfies Him, and that is what we need to know. We don't need to know **how** this happens, only that He says it does.

Error: Christ Wouldn't Prevent His Own Crucifixion. How Can He Help Me?

Another problem for many people in understanding the reliability of the Fatherhood of God is that when Christ was on the cross, He would not accept the challenges and taunting of the crowds to overpower His crucifiers and come down from the cross. In the minds of many people is the thought, "How is Christ going to rescue me from my suffering, if He couldn't even rescue Himself from the crucifixion?" This is a problem that everyone must resolve. The solution to this problem is the concept that time means very little to God. A day is like a thousand years in the mind of God (2 Peter 3:8, Psalms 90:4). Christ refused to rescue Himself from the shame, and scorn, and suffering that He received, but then did something far greater. He rescued Himself from death! Rather than overcoming a handful of Roman soldiers, He overcame death and the devil in a final kind of way that totally changed the history of the world. He refused to do what men would have Him do, in return for doing something far greater than anyone expected Him to do!

This is what I see happening in people's lives today, over and over again. They want more than anything for God to do **this,** or do **that,** their way, but God doesn't do it their way. They conclude that He's never going to rescue them, and that He's never going to meet their needs. Meanwhile, God is making it obvious to anybody who looks objectively at that life that He is trying to do something far greater. The woman whom I mentioned at the beginning of this presentation wanted God to have prevented the accident in which her inner ear was injured. Because He didn't prevent her accident, she became bitter toward Him. She essentially felt that God would never meet her needs. Meanwhile, as a result of her accident, God had led her to a psychiatrist who diagnosed several things that had been marring the quality and goodness and joy and peace in her life. Those emotional problems could have been resolved within approximately three months of weekly therapy. Had she accepted and constructively used the consultation that God provided her, it would have helped both her present problem and the rest of her life. In addition, she had received a revelation from the Lord of His attempting to reach out to her in a very special and personal way. But her bitterness and self pity were blinding her to the Lord, to His love for her, and blinding her to the fact that what God wanted to give to her was even better than what **she** wanted.

Problem: Why Should We Fear God, Who Says That He Loves Us?

Another common problem is the fear of the Lord. The Bible says He loves us as His sons, and that we should love Him. Yet, the Bible says that we should fear Him. This is another intellectual snare for people who merely look at this with ordinary intellectual understanding and without spiritual understanding. Initially, this seems to be contradictory, but it isn't. If you begin looking at the concept of the fear of God with the understanding that God is the perfectly ethical judge of the universe who also loves us, then you can begin to see what the fear of the Lord really means. It means that we must understand that at the same time that God loves us, He cannot break His promises (Numbers 23:19), or sacrifice His perfection, or His perfectly ethical judgeship, for some rotten sin of ours. If He were to let sin go unpunished, we wouldn't have God, we'd have something else. We would have a judge who would be like earthly judges who let murderers, thieves, and rapists escape punishment. What would we have to worship? God doesn't destroy His judgeship, His Godship, His perfectly ethical condition just because we don't like the consequences of our sins. If we will understand that, then we can have a much better understanding of what it means to fear God. It means to fear that God is in the same bind that we're in: He has got to obey His own rules that He has given us. He can't tell us, "You must lead ethical lives and be righteous, and avoid sin," and then proceed to sin Himself, in dealing with us. He can't violate His own rules in trying to minister to us and parent us and meet our needs for spiritual, emotional, and character development.

Proverbs 19:23 says, *"The fear of the Lord tendeth to life: and he that hath it shall abide satisfied; he shall not be visited with evil."* Here is a promise that points to what I have just explained. If a person fears the Lord, he is going to be content. He will avoid sinful behavior, and God will protect him from evil experiences. On the other hand, whenever one engages in evil or sinful behavior, God must do something in response to it. Even though He won't necessarily kill us and cast us into hell, He will have to do something unpleasant in response to sin.

Psalms 34:7-22 offers a series of promises about the fear of the Lord that again emphasize God's protection in return.

"7 - The angel of the Lord encampeth round about them that fear him, and delivereth them.
"8 - Oh taste and see that the Lord is good: blessed is the man that trusteth in him.
"9 - O fear the Lord, ye his saints: for there is no want to them that fear him.
"10 - The young lions do lack, and suffer hunger: but they that seek the Lord shall not want any good thing.
"11 - Come, ye children, harken unto me: I will teach you the fear of the Lord.
"12 - What man is he that desireth Life, and loveth many

days, that he may see good?

"13 - Keep thy tongue from evil, and thy lips from speaking guile.

"14 - Depart from evil, and do good; seek peace and pursue it.

"15 - The eyes of the Lord are upon the righteous, and his ears are open unto their cry.

"16 - The face of the Lord is against them that do evil, to cut off the remembrance of them from the earth.

"17 - The righteous cry, and the Lord heareth, and delivereth them out of all their troubles.

"18 - The Lord is nigh unto them that are of a broken heart; and saveth such as be of a contrite spirit.

"19 - Many are the afflictions of the righteous; but the Lord delivereth him out of them all.

"20 - He keepeth all his bones: not one of them is broken.

"21 - Evil shall slay the wicked: and they that hate the righteous shall be desolate.

"22 - The Lord redeemeth the soul of his servants: and none of them that trust in him shall be desolate."

The Psalm thus explains that the Lord is against the wicked, and that He will protect, preserve, and minister to those who are seeking Him and His ways. The righteous may have trouble, but God will see them through those troubles. Those troublesome experiences will then be used to build character, strength and faith. Though the fear of the Lord may momentarily sound like a dreadful thing, when you see the kinds of promises that the Bible gives in return, you can see that this is only a good thing — only good. One must merely understand that God is in a bind because He is totally ethical. He can't break His own promises, and He can't lie in dealing with any of us, His children.

Emotional Causes of Confusion About The Fatherhood of God

Many emotional problems cause misunderstanding and

confusion about the Fatherhood of God. It is impossible for us to understand God so long as we are falling into the snare of expecting Him to be the same type of Father that our earthly fathers have been. It seems that each of us goes through this. The first gods in our lives, as far as we were concerned as small children, were our parents. These gigantic beings seemed to us to know everything, and seemed able to do everything. The Bible makes it clear that God is our Father. The subconscious mind equates all beings with the name **Father.** We thus go through life subconsciously expecting God to respond to us the same way as our earthly fathers did. This is not so much of a problem to those whose earthly fathers were people who feared the Lord, and who worshipped Him, and who had a proper relationship with God. The characteristics of God will in fact be very similar to those of one's earthly father, if his earthly father tried to reproduce the character of Christ in his own life as Christ taught us to do. On the other hand, it is rare that any of us have had fathers who were that close to the Lord. It is rare that any of us have had fathers who didn't have some real weakness, some real tendency to enter into some particular form of sin which somehow hurt us or let us down during our childhood years. We consequently misperceive God, erroneously expecting Him to have the same emotional and character defects that our earthly fathers demonstrated. We then become bitter towards the Lord because of this, when it is really nothing more than our own subconscious minds playing tricks upon us. This condition is referred to as a negative parental transference toward God. Negative feelings toward an earthly father are subconsciously transferred to God.

The subconscious mind demonstrates a type of illogical reasoning called **predicate thinking,** or **primary process thinking.** This produces negative parental transferences to God. The subconscious mind reasons as follows: "My earthly father didn't care about me. God is a father. Therefore God won't care enough about me either." This

60

erroneous logic of the subconscious is quite a departure from reality. This is the kind of subconscious against which we struggle. If we give in to it, we let our subconscious minds have dominion over our lives, rather than giving God that dominion. We then become victims of that kind of erroneous, illogical thinking.

A woman who was suffering from severe depression and chronic anxiety doubted that God was real. She felt that even if He were real, how could she possibly trust Him? Was there anything more than just negative things to be expected from God? Consequently, why be concerned with God? This woman was in an emotional crisis as well as a spiritual crisis. Every time that an attempt was made to understand her emotional problems, she realized that she felt totally lost, as if she were floating in space with no boundaries, and with nothing that she could use to understand her life or direct it. She had many negative things to say about her earthly father, who had been an alcoholic. She mentioned a long list of things that this man had done during her childhood about which she had been complaining for decades. My mental response to each of those complaints was, "Well, that was what a father **should** have told her. That was a limit that he **should** have set for his child." For example, she bitterly complained, "My father demanded that I stay away and go to college out of state for an extra year beyond what I wished." I said, "Why did your father tell you that?" She replied, "I think that it was something to the effect that he wanted me to grow up." Here she was, over thirty years old, still emotionally immature, in a psychiatrist's office, partly for that reason. I could see the wisdom of what her father had been trying to do, the only way that he knew how.

Another gripe against her father was that he demanded that she not continue to date a particular boy when she was in her late teens. "Well," I asked, "What happened to that guy?" "Oh, he has been in and out of asylums ever since he got out of his teens." I said, "Don't you think that your father must have sensed that there was something bizarre about this person? Don't you think that your father wanted to protect you from what you would have experienced in a permanent relationship with someone in that mental condition?'' ''Well, I never thought of **that**,'' she said. She described a list of other inappropriate attacks upon her father's parenting of her.

A further understanding of her difficulties revealed that very early in her life, her mother had died. On the day that her ailing mother went to the hospital, this small child sensed that her mother was so dreadfully ill, that if she went to the hospital she would die and never come back. As she had feared, her mother did die in the hospital. Decades later, this woman still felt that she had caused her mother's death, because she had not told her mother, "If you go to the hospital, you are going to die." It turned out that the mother had a serious medical condtion for which there was no treatment available at that time. It was inevitable, because of the nature of her condition, that she was highly likely to die. That little girl sensed that her mother was going to die, remained silent about this due to the overwhelming anxiety of this thought, and erroneously concluded that it was the **hospital** rather than the illness which killed her mother.

After her mother's death, the mother's side of the family began to make bitter remarks against the patient's father. They said, "Her husband was responsible for her death. He always made her work too hard and do too many things. That damaged her health and caused her death." There was no truth whatsoever to those remarks. When the child heard that somebody was blaming her father for the death of her mother, she then began thinking to herself, "Well, maybe **father** killed mother. Maybe **I** didn't kill her after all. Maybe **I'm** not really responsible." Throughout her life, she had continued feeling that her father had killed her mother. Consequently, she felt contempt for her father. She then transferred this contempt onto her perception of God. In her mind, fathers were murderers. In fact, fathers were especially likely to kill females, so she had better look out for them.

You can see the tremendous lies that one has to believe in order to reach the conclusion that you can't count on God, or that He is going to do nothing but damage you. It is very impressive to me that God will go so far to try to save us from ourselves. In Matthew, Chapter 18, Verse 14, Christ taught, "Even so it is not the will of your Father, which is in heaven, that one of these little ones should perish."

In John, Chapter 6, in Verses 37 through 40, Christ said, *"37 - All that the Father giveth me shall come to me: and him that cometh to me I will in no wise cast out. 38 - For I came down from heaven, not to do mine own will, but the will of him that sent me. 39 - And this is the Father's will which hath sent me, that of all which he hath given me I should lose nothing, but should raise it up again at the last day. 40 - And this is the will of him that sent me, that every one which seeth the Son, and believeth on him, may have everlasting life: and I will raise him up at the last day."*

Here we're told that not one person whom God wanted Christ to save was lost! For a long time after I first saw this message in the Bible, I wondered, "How does Christ do that? The human condition is an incredibly stubborn one. What kind of miracle does Christ perform to get so many stubborn people back to Him the way He wants us?"

Books such as **Life After Life**[1] and **Reflections On Life After Life,**[2] by Dr. Raymond Moody, have described the experiences of people who had near death experiences during cardiac arrest, and who have been resuscitated. Those people gave testimonies of having had what they felt were clearly encounters with Christ, during the time that their hearts had stopped beating. Many of them described scenes that seemed to be a reproduction of the Bible's description of heaven. None of the people whom Dr. Moody interviewed described hell. For some reason, all of the after-life testimonies that he obtained were of heaven. Dr. Moody is a psychiatrist. He usually interviewed his subjects days, weeks, months, or years following their near death experiences. People began to say, "Aha! There is no hell. You can see from this that the

Bible is wrong."

In 1978, Dr. Maurice Rawlings, a cardiologist, published **Beyond Death's Door.**[3] In it, he described accounts of the near-death experiences of patients whom he attended at the time of their cardiac arrests. Dr. Rawlings discovered that while some people described what they felt were encounters with Christ and heaven, others described experiences identical to the Biblical descriptions of hell, even down to the lake of fire, and tremendous torment. Some of them would yell, "Don't let me stay in hell! Get me out of here!" He was able to resuscitate some, but not others. He noticed that the people who had this type of experience "in hell" could tell you about it for approximately twenty-four hours after it took place. If he waited much longer than that to interview them about their experiences, he found that they had totally repressed the memories of them. Those were such horrible experiences that after a day or so they had absolutely no memory whatsoever of them. Nonetheless, their lives were changed for the better following these experiences.

These near-death experiences reveal the incredible extremes to which God will go in order to save His children from the consequences of hell, even in spite of their own stubbornness and sinfulness. I would have to say that this is miraculous. If nothing else that God does in order to reach us works, He will even cast us into hell momentarily, just for a few moments, in His desperate attempt to try to save us from ourselves, from our own waywardness.

The best way that I can conclude a talk on the Fatherhood of God is by simply sharing one of the many, many promises in the Scriptures that reveal what God our Father wants to give us if we will only receive it. This is Isaiah, Chapter 40:31: *"But they that wait upon the Lord shall renew their strength; they shall mount up with wings as eagles; they shall run, and not be weary; and they shall walk, and not faint."*

Bibliography

1. Moody, Raymond A., Jr., M.D. **Life After Life.** Covington, Georgia: Mockingbird Books, 1975.
2. Moody, Raymond A., Jr., M.D. **Reflections On Life After Life.** New York, New York: Bantam/Mockingbird Books, 1977.
3. Rawlings, Maurice, M.D. **Beyond Death's Door.** Nashville, Tennessee: Thomas Nelson, Inc. Publishers, 1978.

4

Is The Power Of God Part Of Your Life?

Few people seem to realize the importance of placing the **power** of God foremost in thinking about their lives. Even the Apostles and early Christians who had walked with Christ were at times reluctant to believe the power that He would manifest in demonstrating His concern for their lives. We get a glimpse of this in Acts 12:1-24.

"1 - Now about that time Herod the King stretched forth his hands to vex certain of the church.

"2 - And he killed James the brother of John with the sword.

"3 - And because he saw it pleased the Jews, he proceeded further to take Peter also. (Then were the days of unleavened bread.)

"4 - And when he had apprehended him, he put him in prison, and delivered him to four quaternions of soldiers to keep him; intending after Easter to bring him forth to the people.

"5 - Peter therefore was kept in prison: but prayer was made without ceasing of the church unto God for him.

"6 - And when Herod would have brought him forth, the same night Peter was sleeping between two soldiers, bound with two chains: and the keepers before the

door kept the prison.

"7 - And, behold, the angel of the Lord came upon him, and a light shined in the prison: and he smote Peter on the side, and raised him up, saying, Arise up quickly. And his chains fell off from his hands.

"8 - And the angel said unto him, Gird thyself, and bind on thy sandals. And so he did. And he saith unto him, Cast thy garment about thee, and follow me.

"9 - And he went out, and followed him; and wist not that it was true which was done by the angel; but thought he saw a vision.

"10 - When they were past the first and the second ward, they came unto the iron gate that leadeth unto the city; which opened to them of his own accord: and they went out, and passed on through one street; and forthwith the angel departed from him.

"11 - And when Peter was come to himself, he said, Now I know of a surety that the Lord hath sent his angel, and hath delivered me out of the hand of Herod, and from all the expectation of the people of the Jews.

"12 - And when he had considered the thing, he came to the house of Mary the mother of John, whose surname was Mark; where many were gathered together praying.

"13 - And as Peter knocked at the door of the gate, a damsel came to hearken, named Rhoda.

"14 - And when she knew Peter's voice, she opened not the gate for gladness, but ran in, and told how Peter stood before the gate.

"15 - And they said unto her, Thou art mad. But she constantly affirmed that it was even so. Then said they, It is his angel.

"16 - But Peter continued knocking: and when they had opened the door, and saw him, they were astonished.

"17 - But he, beckoning unto them with the hand to hold their peace, declared unto them how the Lord had brought him out of the prison. And he said, Go shew

*these things unto James, and to the brethren. And he
departed, and went into another place.*

*"18 - Now as soon as it was day, there was no small stir
among the soldiers, what was become of Peter.*

*"19 - And when Herod had sought for him, and found him
not, he examined the keepers, and commanded that
they should be put to death. And he went down from
Judea to Caesarea, and there abode.*

*"20 - And Herod was highly displeased with them of Tyre
and Sidon: but they came with one accord to him,
and, having made Blastus the king's chamberlain
their friend, desired peace; because their country was
nourished by the king's country.*

*"21 - And upon a set day Herod, arrayed in royal apparel,
sat upon his throne, and made an oration unto them.*

*"22 - And the people gave a shout, saying, It is the voice of
a god, and not a man.*

*"23 - And immediately the angel of the Lord smote him,
because he gave not God the glory: and he was eaten
up of worms, and gave up the ghost.*

"24 - But the word of God grew and multiplied."

These Scriptures give us a glimpse of the limited
expectations of prayer that even the disciples of the early
Christian Church experienced. Though they were praying
without ceasing for the release of Peter from prison, when the
prayer was answered, their initial reaction was one of
disbelief. All of us go through this at times in our lives. We
pray for something, and wish that it would take place. But
down deep in our hearts, there is a doubt about just how
powerful God is, just how knowledgeable He is about our
needs, or just how much He cares about us and the many
situations in which we need His help. Peter was imprisoned
under maximum security, with chains and guards on either
side and all about him. The only way that he could get out of
that prison was by the Lord intervening and releasing him as
was done through His angel.

68

Any undesirable situation from which you cannot personally release yourself is a prison. Everyone is at times in a prison created by the situations and circumstances of his life. You may have experienced hard times in your past, when no matter what you did, you couldn't release yourself from the imprisonment of prolonged, painful circumstances. You may even be in that kind of prison now, in some area of your life. Perhaps it's a disastrous marital, financial, health, or job problem. Some distressing situation may entrap our lives for weeks, months, or even years before we can be released from it. When we look to what happened to the disciples and look at their disbelief, we can see our own problems and disbelief. We may pray, and yet may feel some doubt about just what God will do. Questions may arise in our minds, such as, "Just how much does He really care about me?"

People often have to obtain psychiatric help, because there is some reason why they won't use their personal relationships with God to stabilize themselves in the situations which exist in their lives. Something is lacking in their relationships with Christ. The most common reason that I see for the inability of many people to put their Christianity to work when they are in difficult, troubled situations is that in their hearts they aren't giving God credit for the power that He really has, even when He manifests Himself and His power to them.

When Peter went into that prison, the Bible says that he went to sleep that night. I am sure that most of us would not have been able to sleep very well in that situation, but Peter did. We must ask, "When did God get the power to release each of us from the bad or difficult circumstances that may imprison our lives at a given time?" Did God get the power to release Peter shortly before he entered that prison, or at the moment that he was placed in prison, or a day, a week, or a month later? When did God get that power? Most people would acknowledge that God had the power to release Peter before he ever entered that prison. As a matter of fact, we can see why God put him into that prison. He put him in there to reveal Himself — His power, His concern, His love, and His responsiveness to prayer — to Peter, to the disciples, and to us today. He revealed Himself in a way that would strengthen the faith of those Christians. In their future lives and ministries, they would know from experience what the power of God was like.

The average person who finds himself imprisoned by an uncomfortable or painful life situation doesn't believe anything that I have said up until now. The average person who starts praying to God to release him from an imprisoning situation refuses to consider the following important spiritual truths. God had the power and knowledge to release him from that situation before it occurred. God chose neither to prevent it nor to immediately release him from it. God permitted the occurrence of each situation that we face, and He has the power to release us from it at the time that He knows is the **right** time for what He is trying to build in our lives. Most people will not acknowledge that. They want to say that God is only going to provide what is good in **their** opinions, what is comfortable in **their** opinions, what seems right to **them** at the moment. They overlook the concept that God frequently reveals Himself through very painful, confining situations, probably because nothing else will change us in the necessary ways. Most people don't want to look at the idea that God has the power to release them at the moment they enter a painful situation, because then they have to face the idea that God somehow caused it. Their own personal shortcomings, carelessness, or ungodliness may have created the situation. They may deserve it, because of previous sinful behavior. Nonetheless, because God has the power to release one from a painful situation at any time, it is necessary to look to God as providing that situation.

Once we begin giving God credit for having the power to release us from a situation even before it begins, we can then begin asking questions like, "Well, Lord, what are you trying to build in my life by placing me in this situation? What is it that you are trying to tear down in my life and rebuild in a different and better way, as you know it needs to be?'' But don't you see that you can't possibly ask those questions unless you first give God credit even for what is painful and for what you don't like? If God is trying to turn our lives around, He has a concept of what our lives should become. We may be a long way from that. Then God's primary concern is what He is trying to make us become, not merely what we are now, not merely what feels good now. What might feel good to us and what we might choose right now might very well keep us in the same old rut without any character building or closer relationship with God whatsoever. In order for any real or important changes to occur in our lives, some tearing down is often necessary before any rebuilding can begin. Just as a building can usually not be remodeled without first doing some tearing down, a personality usually cannot be rebuilt without first tearing down some of the old self. That tearing down hurts. It is always painful. I am going to present a few brief examples of people who were at times unable to apply their relationships with Christ in facing difficult situations, as a result of their reluctance to acknowledge His power, even after He had revealed it.

A woman who had experienced a lengthy battle with a very deadly form of cancer had been healed. She told me that at the time her remission occurred, Christ made a personal appearance and told her that her cancer was in remission before her physicians discerned this. When the doctors subsequently confirmed that the cancer was in remission, she told them she knew that already. She now found herself in a psychiatrist's office, because she needed strength to face any future bad news that might occur regarding her health, such as if the cancer were to recur. She found that each time in the past that she had a setback in her battle with cancer, she had to resort to smoking. She had found it very difficult to break the smoking habit each time that she resumed it. She wanted the strength to be able to face whatever her future might hold, without having to resort to cigarettes. My immediate

71

reaction to that was, "In order to give up the cigarettes, you will need something that is much more effective with which to face whatever your future holds." My thought was that she needed to become able to put her relationship with Christ to work in her life. Christ was apparently already reaching out to her. She needed to be able to respond in a more successful way. Then I asked the question, "What are your thoughts about why God permitted you to have that cancer?"

Most people do not want to look at the possibility that God permits or causes disease. They feel disease must be exclusively of Satan. Yet, God makes it clear throughout the Bible that He maintains dominion over Satan. When God called Moses out of the desert to deliver the enslaved Jews from Egypt, Moses objected. Exodus 4:10-12 describes this:

> *"10 - And Moses said unto the Lord, O my Lord, I am not eloquent, neither heretofore, nor since thou hast spoken unto thy servant: but I am slow of speech, and of a slow tongue.*
> *"11 - And the Lord said unto him, Who hath made man's mouth? or who maketh the dumb, or deaf, or the seeing, or the blind? Have not I the Lord?*
> *"12 - Now therefore go, and I will be with thy mouth, and teach thee what thou shalt say."*

Why does God permit a person to have cancer? If He knew beforehand that Peter was about to be imprisoned, and He had the power to release Peter from prison before Peter got into the prison, then God wanted Peter in that prison for a time. This woman became very upset with me, and told me that she didn't want to hear that sort of thing. This interaction taught me why she was experiencing present emotional difficulty. She told me that Christ Himself had made a personal appearance to her. She had no history of psychosis, and I had no reason to think that she was out of touch with reality. I was satisfied that this had taken place. She had communicated to me, "Look, I want you to know that Christ healed my cancer. Not only did He heal it, but he **told** me that he healed it." But now she was telling me, "Don't tell me that Christ caused my cancer! He healed it years after it began. But He didn't cause it." What she was communicating subconsciously, and what she was **believing** subconsciously, was this: "When my cancer began, Christ had nothing to do with it. He had nothing to do with it, because He may have been unperceptive, or uninformed, and didn't know that I had cancer. Or maybe He didn't care about my having that cancer then. Or, maybe He knew all about it and was concerned about me, but He didn't have enough power at the moment that that cancer began to stop it." That was the subconscious reasoning in her mind. Basically, she was doing what many of us have done at times in these types of imprisoning situations. She was subconsciously telling herself that Christ did not have the power, love, and concern to stop her cancer at the moment it began; but years later, He somehow came up with the wherewithal to stop it. Because this woman was self contradicting what she really believed about Christ's power, love, and wisdom, she really could not place any **faith** in Christ, not even after His personal appearance! The Bible is filled with accounts of people to whom God made personal appearances, and to whom that subsequently wasn't sufficient. They still didn't trust Him. Even after what she felt was a personal appearance of Christ, this woman couldn't place her faith in Christ's ability to handle whatever situation she might face.

My immediate question was, "Why did Christ permit this person to have cancer?" I believe in the power of God, the wisdom of God, and the love of God. When I asked this in faith, it was easy for me to see some of the things that Christ was probably trying to change in that woman's life. This particular individual had a greatly overgrown self-will, combined with an extremely high intelligence; and she wouldn't listen to anyone. She was not amenable to counsel. She generally used her intelligence to let others know that she felt that they were inadequate beside her. These were very problematic qualities of her personality. When a high intelligence is combined with a blinding self-will, there is no limit to the amount of trouble that one can create for himself and others. Such personalities inflict an incredible amount of unhappiness upon themselves and other people. I could easily see how everything that this woman had been through in the way of pain, suffering, and fear, would have been worth the beneficial changes that Christ was probably trying to produce in her personality.

This person might have responded to her situation by saying, "Lord, I'm going to look at what you're trying to do in my life. I'm going to try to fully understand what you are trying to change in me, what you are trying to build in me. Whatever you are trying to do has got to be the right thing for my life. I accept whatever you want to do in my life: whatever you want to build, and whatever you want to tear down and rebuild, because you know that it is the best thing for my life." This woman demonstrated a total lack of any of those concepts. She was only concerned with relying upon her exaggerated self-will to deal with future situations. She consequently had to rely on the tobacco addiction to get her through any tribulation regarding her health. Whenever one fails to acknowledge the sovereignity of God in thinking about his life, he must then rely upon something else. Though this woman's situation was somewhat extreme, it is nonethless very typical. She was imprisoned by the cancer that was usually incurable, with statistically horrible cure rates. Though Christ healed that incurable cancer, she would not trust Him because of her refusal to acknowledge His dominion over the cancer and over her body at the moment that the cancer began. Though her Christianity may be of value in the afterlife, it seemed of little use in this life, because of her self-contradictory tendency.

This concept that Christ may be responsible for unpleasant things that take place in our lives is frightening to many people. Yet, if He lets something occur, and fails to stop it,

74

He must have willed it, even if it is painful. The application of this concept to situations makes it easy to put your Christianity to work. I don't know of any other way to really put it to work. Other than that, it becomes an abstract system of armchair philosophy that may be interesting, but not helpful in everyday life. The Bible clearly tells us that God has power over every dimension of our lives, and over Satan.

A highly successful businessman was situationally imprisoned by extensive burns which confined him to a hosptial bed for several months. He responded to his injury by emotionally regressing to the status of a helpless, demanding child who felt and acted as though he could do nothing for himself, not even mentally. He demanded that someone remove all of his pain, while he totally refused to even try the self hypnosis which was taught him for pain relief. He presented the emotional picture of a child having a temper tantrum. His emotional responses were severely immature compared to those of the average person whom I have seen with a similar extent of burns. He often got into verbal fights with all of his physicians at the same time that he begged them to help him. In the course of seeing him, I asked at one point, "What are your thoughts about why God let you get burned?" He said, "I know why God did that. I've always hated doctors, ever since I was a kid. If a doctor ever called me up in my business, I wouldn't even return his call. Now I'm in here having to get to know doctors, to find out what some of them are really like, and to have them take care of me." I asked, "Why did you hate doctors so much?" He said, "When I was a kid, my mother was a terrible hypochondriac. Her 'thing' was to act as though she were about to die with a heart attack. Anytime I did anything she disliked, she would start to 'die' with a heart attack, telling me it was my fault that she was going to die, and that I was the one who had killed her. As soon as she would start that act, she would get on the phone and call up her doctor. I just came to hate doctors, because this scene took place over and over, throughout my childhood. I was constantly

75

overwhelmed with guilt and worry, feeling that I had to do anything that she wanted, no matter how irrational it might be, or else she would begin 'dying with a heart attack' and would call a doctor.''

This man had a multitude of problems which needed to be resolved, but the main thing that he really needed to do was to make peace with doctors. He also needed to make peace with his mother regarding all of the bitterness that was locked inside his heart over all those years of trauma. He needed to do some extremely important personality rebuilding regarding his perception of both himself and others. All of the trouble that he had to go through to recover from those burns would have been worth it, had he made the changes that needed to be made in his personality. Unfortunately he didn't do that. When he learned that I was a Christian, he used that as an excuse to fire me. This was a poorly disguised decision to continue acting upon his irrational bitterness rather than to resolve it.

Another man had the surgical scar from a corrected hare lip. In his adult life, he wore a mustache which concealed the scar. During his childhood, that scar had been quite apparent, and he had received a good deal of teasing from other children. I asked him, ''What did God build in your life through that hare lip? What are your thoughts about why He let that happen?'' He replied, ''God built a lot of things in my life through this. He taught me compassion and an understanding of the feelings of other people, that I would never have learned in any other way.'' This man had used those character strengths that had resulted from that hare lip in order to develop an extremely successful career which involved meeting large numbers of people. Had you seen him being teased during childhood for his hare lip scar, you might never have stopped to consider that God was building something good through that. You would have had to wait decades later and to see and understand the final product.

A woman who had been labelled **retarded** during her childhood, sought consultation decades later for depression.

The depression had resulted from years of thinking that she was always going to be a retarded individual who would never accomplish good or desirable things. She experienced a learning disability during childhood for which she was placed in special education classes. Special efforts were expended upon her in order for her to learn what others could learn with no struggle. I asked, "What was God trying to build in you by letting you have that learning disability during your childhood?" Well, the answer was easy. This individual had struggled faithfully through all of those years of being mislabeled as **inadequate, stupid, dumb, retarded, unable to learn.** She had simply done the best that she could. She was now a successful college student. She had discovered that because of her compassion for retarded children, she could teach them with unusual effectiveness. She had worked as an assistant teacher of retarded children. She was successfully studying social work so that she could one day counsel retarded children and those with other learning disabilities. The average person doesn't want to be around retarded children, and mentally de-values such work. This young woman now had the kind of compassion that was vitally needed for working effectively with people of this type. When she replaced her bitterness with thankfulness for what God had already begun to do through her past experience, she was healed of her depression.

In Matthew 10:29-31, Christ teaches, *"Are not two sparrows sold for a farthing? and one of them shall not fall on the ground without your Father. 30 - But the very hairs of your head are all numbered. 31 - Fear ye not therefore, ye are of more value than many sparrows."*

Christ made it clear that God knows everything about us. In examining the life histories of many people, it has been obvious to me that this teaching is unquestionably true. God is aware of each problem that we face, and He is building character strengths in us which are the end results of tribulation. The outcomes of these experiences are often so valuable, that only the Divine Creator could have designed such experiences.

The Second Epistle of Paul to Timothy, 3:1-5 prophesies a coming age of apostacy (turning away from the faith) in which people will pretend to be godly, but will deny the power of God. *"This know also, that in the last days perilous times shall come. 2 - For men shall be lovers of their own selves, covetous, boasters, proud, blastphemers, disobedient to parents, unthankful, unholy. 3 - Without natural affection, trucebreakers, false accusers, incontinent, fierce, despisers of those that are good, 4 - Traitors, heady, high minded, lovers of pleasures more than lovers of God; 5 - Having a form of godliness, but denying the power thereof: from such turn away."*

It seems likely that Verse 5 presents the cause of the ungodly condition of many lives: the individuals deny the **power** of God! It is natural that one would mentally minimize the **importance** of God in proportion to his tendency to mentally minimize the **power** of God in his life.

On the other hand, those who are willing to look for the power of God in their lives will see it, for the Bible promises that God manifests Himself to all men (Romans 1:19). In Matthew 19:26 Christ promises, *"With God all things are possible."*

5

The Power Of The
Spoken Word
Of Man And God

The quality of our lives is not determined as much by what happens to us as it is determined by what we say to ourselves and others about those situations. A person's attitude consists of what he says to himself. We are constantly talking to ourselves mentally, and the things that we say to ourselves have a crucial effect on what we experience. People are constantly saying things to themselves such as the following. "I can," or "I can't." "I love," or "I hate." "I trust God," or "I must worry all the time." "I'm bad," or "I'm good." They may be engaging in self pity, saying, "Poor me. God won't give me what I want," versus *"God will meet all of my needs* (Philippians 4:19)." Each of these mental statements are attitudes which produce either peace or despair. *"God has forgiven me of my confessed sins* (1 John 1:9)," versus "God will never forgive me." "I must constantly worry about when I'm going to die," or *"I need have no concern about that, for God will appoint the time of my death* (Ecclesiastes 3:2)." "I hate my parents, I am my parents, and I hate myself," versus "I forgive my parents for hurting me, and I can be different from them in those ways which would be best." "Everyone will know how no good I am and will reject me," versus "Anyone who knows me will see the love and character of Christ reflected through me." "I am bound to fail in whatever I try," versus "In Christ I can do all things." The attitudes which we put into our minds determine the emotions which our minds emit.

When the words of a person to himself or others contradict the words of God in the Bible, the resulting attitudes produce anxiety, depression, disability, or despair. When a person's words to himself or others agree with the words of God, the resulting attitudes produce peace, joy, and fruitfulness.

Proverbs 18:21 says, "Death and life are in the power of the tongue: and they that love it shall eat the fruit thereof." That is a tremendously important statement — death and life are somehow determined by what we say. It is being realized more and more in many areas of study, that attitudes determine the state of one's physical health. In the book, **Type A Behavior And Your Heart**[1] Drs. Friedman and Rosenman show that a person's attitude and tendency to "fly off the handle" very easily can cause premature heart attacks. Therapeutic radiologist Dr. Carl Simonton and his wife, Stephanie, who work in Fort Worth, Texas, have statistically demonstrated that certain personality characteristics are correlated with susceptibility to highly malignant diseases.[2] Furthermore, of those people who have malignancies, the ones likely to recover can be predicted by their attitudes. The Simontons have discovered that the person who is highly likely to die of cancer is characteristically chronically bitter, has little if any ability to forgive, has a low self image, and is likely to engage in self pity. They have also determined that cancer patients with the above troublesome personality characteristics may have less than a 50% chance to be cured. Yet, when these troublesome personality characteristics have been reversed with counselling, far more than the statistically expected number of these patients recovered and survived.

The attending physician of a woman who had been burned over half her body requested that I teach her to mentally control the pain and the anguish from daily dressing changes during which the dressings had to be literally ripped off.

After successfully using techniques of concentration and mental distraction to completely anesthetize herself as needed for three weeks, she suddenly became unable to do this. When I explored the reason for the sudden failure in an interview with her, it was discovered that she was not able to tolerate the success that she had been experiencing. She had never envisioned herself as a successful person. Merely recovering from that much injury made it necessary for her to be extremely successful. Her success with pain control had won her the praise and admiration of her physical therapists, nurses, and acquaintances. She was also having a terrible problem healing. For some reason, she took over twice as long as an average person would need to heal any given size of wound. Once she realized that her main problem had been her visualizing herself as an unsuccessful person who couldn't even be successful to heal or to control her thoughts, she again began anesthetizing herself, and even healing properly. She told me many times during her hospitalization that she felt that she would have died had it not been for the work that we did together! A year after she was discharged from the hospital, I saw her accidentally in public, and she told me the same thing: "You know, I have always felt that I would have died when I was in that hospital if it wouldn't have been for the work that we did." What we did consisted of reversing her attitude. She had reversed the habit of telling herself constantly, "I can't make it. I can't make it. I can't succeed. I can't succeed." The reversal of what she had been doing with her tongue had most likely made the difference between death and life for her, just as Proverbs 18:21 says!

People sometimes lose their mental health because of agreeing with negativistic, spoken words of their parents, and because of what they then begin telling themselves in response. So reliable is the tongue as an index of what is in the mind, that the spoken words of patients are the primary means of psychiatric diagnosis. In the practice of psychiatry, I very rarely use psychological tests. I rarely need to obtain any kind of physical or laboratory examinations. I just listen to what people say. From what they say, I can usually determine what is in the subconscious mind.

The Bible's statements about the **heart** are clearly truths about what we now refer to as the subconscious mind. Christ knew that what comes out of the mouth is a reflection of the attitudes which exist in the subconscious mind. In Matthew 15:18-19, Christ said, *"But those things which proceed out of the mouth come forth from the heart; and they defile the man. 19 For out of the heart proceed evil thoughts, murders, adulteries, fornications, thefts, false witness, blastphemies."*

In Matthew 12:34, Christ told the Pharisees, *"O generation of vipers, how can ye, being evil, speak good things? For out of the abundance of the heart the mouth speaketh."* Here Christ again revealed His understanding of the connection between a man's words and what is in his inner mind.

The entire third chapter of James has a great deal to say about the power of the tongue, the spoken word, to affect lives. I will present just a few selected verses of that chapter here.

"2 - For in many things we offend all. If any man offend not in word, the same is a perfect man, and able also to bridle the whole body." Here the Bible is teaching that if a man can control his tongue, he can control his entire body. Physicians see the truth of this in their daily practice of medicine and psychiatry. People work themselves up into a frenzy of anxiety and depression, merely by mentally giving themselves negative suggestions. The depression and anxiety then cause peptic ulcers, high blood pressure, strokes, or premature heart attacks. The Bible continues teaching in the third chapter of James as follows:

"6 - And the tongue is a fire, a world of iniquity: so is the tongue among our members, that it defileth the whole body, and setteth on fire the course of nature; and it is set on fire of hell."

"8 - But the tongue can no man tame; it is an unruly evil, full of deadly poison."

82

I was once asked to see a middle aged man who was hospitalized with what appeared to be a generalized collapse of his health. His physicians had diagnosed two different types of arthritis which had affected every joint in his body. He also had severe gastrointestinal problems. His facial appearance (acne rosacea) was typical of alcoholism, and he had a beer belly. For many years he had been chronically depressed, chronically bitter. In spite of a very limited education, he held an extremely well paying job. He supervised approximately $1,000,000 worth of business for his company every week. His salary was higher than that of many men who had graduated from college. Nonetheless, his attitude was, "I'm getting too old to ride motorcycles, parachute out of airplanes, or to participate in many other physical activities as I did in the past." He had previously been a tradesman whose work involved a high level of physical risk and physical activity. The fact that he now held such an important supervisory position with such good pay was of no value to him. In his mind, the only thing of value was being some type of superman. Physical performance was the only thing of importance to him, and he was getting too old to do that. In addition, the chronic depression caused by his attitude was making him perhaps fifty years older physiologically and functionally then he was chronologically as a result of his arthritic joint damage. Arthritis is a common complication of chronic depression as well as of obesity. This man was agnostic. His main god was his already declining physical abilities. He rejected both spiritual and psychiatric counsel, choosing instead to continue destroying his life with unrealistic attitudes. This is an illustration of Proverbs 10:11, *"The lips of the righteous feed many, but fools die for want of wisdom."* It is not unusual for a person's foolish words to himself to cause premature loss of health and even death!

It is quite impressive to observe how effectively one's attitude, his spoken words to himself, can cause a loss of his health. Replacing health damaging attitudes or words with the word of God dramatically restores good health. Proverbs

12, Verse 18, says, *"There is that speaketh like the piercings of a sword: but the tongue of the wise is health."* The 13th Proverb in Verses 2 and 3 says, *"A man shall eat good by the fruit of his mouth. . . . 3 - He that keepeth his mouth keepeth his life: but he that openeth wide his lips shall have destruction."*

A young Christian mother sought consultation for anxiety and depression which had been steadily progressing in severity. Her history revealed a behavior pattern of repetitively damaging her life. She had previously dropped out of college, and was currently destroying her relationship with her husband as means of damaging herself. Little wonder that she was anxious and depressed! She never knew what she would do next, in conformity with this compulsion to damage herself. She had no idea what was causing this problem.

During a rapid analysis of this compulsion, she realized that she had been masochistically punishing herself for guilt about premarital sex, smoking, and drinking. I asked if she had confessed those sins. Yes. Did she realize that God promises to forgive confessed sins (1 John 1:9)? Yes. Then why had she not accepted God's forgiveness? Answer: "I don't feel I deserve it, because I am a sinner, and I still sin." I told her that it is quite likely that none of us deserves God's forgiveness. He doesn't forgive us because we deserve it, but because of His love and His promises. I suggested that she consider God's position regarding our confessed sins in the light of the following Biblical truths.

1 - We inherited the sin tendency which afflicted Adam and Eve when they ingested the "fruit" of the tree of knowledge of good and evil, whatever it was.

2 - The Bible says that after they ate that fruit, God told them that the effects of it would thus affect all of mankind. God thus knew this, and had three possible choices in response.

A - He could have immediately destroyed Adam

84

and Eve, thus preventing the proliferation of the sinful human race any further.

B - He could have immediately reversed the sin tendency in Adam and Eve and cleansed their genes of this problem so that it would not be transmitted to all the rest of mankind.

C - He could forgive us for our confessed sins and use our experiences with sinfulness to build character strength in us and to demonstrate to us the necessity for a proper relationship with God. Apparently, His decision to sacrifice His own son for the sins of man made it ethically possible for God to choose this approach.

She found these concepts completely acceptable. At that point, I asked whether she now felt ready to accept God's forgiveness. She did. I suggested that she silently confess all of her sins to God, **receive** the forgiveness of Christ, and let me know when this was accomplished. She did so. The outcome was that her depression lifted and she rejected the compulsion to chronically obtain punishment.

James 1:26 says, *"If any man among you seem to be religious, and bridleth not his tongue, but deceiveth his own heart, this man's religion is vain."* It is an obvious truth that a man could stay in church around the clock; but if he is not bridling his tongue he may be constantly mouthing destructive things to himself, such as telling himself, "I'm an unforgiven sinner who is going to hell." A man can go to church and even confess his sins. If he isn't bridling his tongue, he is not aligning what he is saying with what God says. James' statement that such religion will be in vain is obviously true in this lifetime.

The 21st Proverb, Verse 23 says, *"Whoso keepeth his mouth and his tongue keepeth his soul from troubles."* The word **soul** in the Bible often refers to the mind. Taking this verse in that context, the message is that whoever controls what he says, controls his mind and keeps his mind from

85

being troubled. This basic truth is observed daily in the practice of psychiatry. The individual who habitually says negativistic things to himself and to others regarding his abilities begins to feel and act like an inferior person. He then feels trapped by his **inferiority complex,** which becomes an obstacle to every goal that he pursues. The same individual who responds to counsel by replacing such negative statements to himself and others with positive statements, suddenly replaces his chronic depression, anxiety, and failure patterns with peace, joy, and fruitfulness.

In Ephesians 4:31 the Bible says, *"Let all bitterness, and wrath, and anger, and clamour, and evil speaking, be put away from you, with all malice."* Following these instructions produces emotional health. Failure to do so results in depression, which occurs when bitterness or anger toward others becomes turned inward upon oneself. Dwelling on evil thoughts or evil words produces bitterness and then depression. In Proverbs 15:23 Solomon writes, *"A man hath joy by the answer of his mouth: and a word spoken in due season, how good is it!"* People are looking all about for joy and peace; the Bible has a great deal to say about these two things. Here, in this 15th Proverb, the Bible is saying that you can find joy by what you say. That is very true. People who demonstrate the emotional habit of telling themselves happy, optimistic things are happy. Those who wallow around in self pity and negative suggestions to themselves enter depression and despair.

The Word of God

We have seen a glimpse of the powerful effects of the word of man to produce disease or health in accordance with whether a man's word contradicts or reproduces the word of God. Let us now look at some additional effects of the word of God.

The Word Of God Protects Us From The Sinfulness Of Ourselves And Others

The 17th Psalm, Verse 4 says, *"Concerning the works of men, by the word of thy lips I have kept me from the paths of the destroyer."* Here David is saying that by the word of God, he has kept himself safe from the behavior of violent men. The Bible makes it clear that King David had many enemies who tried repetitively to destroy him. Yet, he lived to be an old man, and died a natural death.

Psalm 119, Verse 11 says, *"Thy word have I hid in mine heart, that I might not sin against thee."* Here is a promise that the word of God will protect one from engaging in sinful behavior.

The Word Of God Produces Peace To Those Who Love It

Psalm 119, Verse 165 says, *"Great peace have they which love thy law; and nothing shall offend them."* Here is a promise of peace for those who love God's law, which is part of His word. Those who love God's laws will follow them. God's laws are perfectly designed to protect us from the evil consequences of ungodly attitudes or behavior. God's laws are also His instructions for obtaining the best that we can have in this life: peace, joy, and fruitfulness.

Proverbs 30:5 says, *"Every word of God is pure: he is a shield unto them that put their trust in him."* Here is a promise of protection for placing our trust in God and His word. The entire 91st Psalm is a lengthy promise of protection to those who rely primarily upon God for protection in any situation. I have heard many testimonies of miraculous survival of circumstances which seemed to offer certain death, when the individuals involved claimed the promises in this Psalm.

The Word of God Produces Power And Understanding

I have seen how true and powerful God's word is when it is

applied in desperate, human situations. In Hebrews 4:12, the Bible says, *"For the word of God is quick, and powerful, and sharper than any two edged sword, piercing even to the dividing asunder of soul and spirit, and of the joints and marrow, and is a discerner of the thoughts and intents of the heart."* I have seen the word of God to be more powerful than a surgeon's scapel. Many people whom I have seen in consultation couldn't be healed by surgeons and internists, but became healed by aligning what they had been saying to themselves with what God has said in the Bible about their lives.

The word of God is the discerner of the thoughts and intents of the heart. If you want to discover someone's attitude about God, himself, or others, start talking to him about the Bible. You will rapidly discover just where He stands in all of these aspects of life. You will quickly see whether he has totally rejected God, whether he is searching for God, or whether he values his relationship with God and a godly life. Contemptible, scornful attitudes toward others, such as "those hypocrites" often indicate self hatred and bitterness toward everyone. Low self image may be reflected by one's conviction that neither God nor others will respect, like, or love him. You can find out such things very quickly, simply by beginning to talk to people about God and the Bible.

The Word Of God Produces Healing

Divine healing is a very complex and controversial subject. Some people believe that God doesn't heal anymore, that only nature heals. Many are ignorant of the conditions which the Bible teaches must be met before God answers prayers, such as confessing any unconfessed sins, demonstrating faith, and seeking a righteous life. James 5:15-16 says, *"And the prayer of faith shall save the sick. . . . 16 - Confess your faults one to another, and pray one for another, that ye may be healed. The effectual fervent prayer of a righteous man availeth much."*

Many people pray for healing with no thought of whether they have really met God's conditions for answering prayer. This often results in unanswered prayer and confusion about the subject of divine healing. I want to share this experience from my family life, because it was so impressive to me, and it is representative of many similar experiences that I have had. My daughter, Michelle, was participating in a cooking lesson one night at age seven, and she accidentally burned her forearm. The bright, red burn was about the size of the palm of her hand. She was quite frightened, because it was very painful. I was sitting nearby, and she came over, wanting me to do something for her. I sat her on my lap and asked her to close her eyes and picture herself relaxing. I urged her to visualize herself placing that arm into a bucket of ice water, and to visualize it completely **normal**. Then I asked if it were alright for us to have prayer together, and she said, "Yes."

The scriptural grounds for the ensuing prayers are as follows:

Matthew 21:21-22
> "21 - *Jesus answered and said unto them, Verily I say unto you, If ye have faith, and doubt not, ye shall not only do this which is done to the fig tree, but also if ye shall say unto this mountain, Be thou removed, and be thou cast into the sea; it shall be done.*
> "22 - *And all things, whatsoever ye shall ask in prayer, believing, ye shall receive.*"

Matthew 18:19
> "19 - *Again I say unto you, that if two of you shall agree on earth as touching any thing that they shall ask, it shall be done for them of my Father which is in heaven.*"

John 14:13-14
> "13 - *And whatsoever ye shall ask in my name, that will I*

do, that the Father may be glorified in the Son.
"14 - If ye ask anything in my name, I will do it."

James 4:7
*"7 - Submit yourselves therefore to God. Resist the devil,
and he will flee from you."*

Luke 10:19
*"Behold, I give you power to tread on serpents and
scorpions, and over all the power of the enemy: and
nothing shall by any means hurt you."*

Matthew 8:17
*"That it might be fulfilled which was spoken by Esaias the
prophet, saying, Himself took our infirmities, and
bare our sicknesses."* (Also see Isaiah 53:4, 1 Peter
2:24)

I began in prayer with my daughter, "Father, we come to
you in the name of Jesus Christ. You know that this child has
burned her arm. We are presenting this arm to you, and we
are asking you to heal it. We command in the name of Jesus
that Satan and all of his representatives be bound and
removed from this arm. We believe that you have healed it."
She was believing her arm was healed, because she was
visualizing it completely normal. I chose to believe that it was
healed by decision. I continued, "Lord, you have promised
that whatsoever we ask believing that we have received it, it
will be given to us. We believe that it is healed, we thank you
for it, we praise you for it."
I then asked her to open her eyes, and we looked at her
arm. In the course of less than one minute, that bright, red
burn completely disappeared! It had to be a hefty burn to
produce that much redness on her olive skin. It completely
went away! I was so impressed by this, that one and a half
hours later, I asked her, "Would you let me see your arm
again?" She looked at it and said, "Daddy, I can't remember

90

which arm I burned!'' I remembered which one it was, and I saw that there was really no difference whatsoever in the appearance of her two arms. This was a fulfillment of Christ's promise in Mark 11:24 (Revised Standard Version), *"Therefore I tell you, whatever you ask in prayer, believe that you have received it, and it will be yours."* It is interesting to me that ths statement is placed in the past tense by many translations of the Bible. Other translations, such as the Modern Language Bible and the Good News Bible also read, *". . . believe that you have received it. . . ."* The Jerusalem Bible reads, *". . . believe that you have it already, and it will be yours."*

This verse has emphasized to me that faith is often something that one can demonstrate by decision. The Bible makes it clear that there is a great deal of faith that comes from the Lord, which is a gift of the Holy Spirit. But there is also an important aspect of faith that is a simple matter of decision. It is a matter of saying, "I am not going to worry about what I see, or what I feel, or what I experience, I am going to believe the word of God rather than anything else in this particular matter. I am placing my trust in His word, and I am acting upon that word now." There are times when one may do that, and it doesn't work. One reason may be that the individual in prayer is involved in some sort of sin that is making the Lord deaf to the prayer. It may also be that God wants to teach that person additional spiritual and psychological truths by means of his illness and recovery before healing him.

Another impressive example of the word of God to heal was demonstrated in the life of a very successful businessman who had to fly internationally in order to perform his job duties. He was on the verge of becoming vocationally incapacitated because of the fear of flying. He had begun doing progressively less work in order to avoid air travel. He was completely unaware of any reason whatsoever for his fear. A rapid analysis of his fear of flying revealed that it was caused by his feeling that he had to control everything. When

91

he was a passenger in an airplane, he didn't control what happened to the plane. Consequently, he was afraid that the plane would crash, and that he would die. His fear of flying was immediately eliminated when he was told that in the Book of Ecclesiastes 3:1-2, the Bible says that **God** will appoint the time to die. I pointed out that he was not responsible for when he was going to die, and there was no need to worry about it. It was God's problem. God had all that in control. It wasn't even up to the pilot. He didn't have to worry about what the pilot was doing or about trusting the pilot with his life. It wasn't the pilot's problem at all — it was God's problem. That turned this man's life around. I later saw him two and a half years later for a marital problem that was completely irrelevant to the fear of flying. He had been flying internationally with no problem at all ever since I had last seen him. This is an example of the tremendous power of God's word to produce health, compared to this man's opposing word, which had produced illness and incapacitation.

Effects Of The Spoken Word On The Lives Of Biblical People

I would like to reflect briefly upon several Biblical people whose lives were greatly affected by their attitudes. I will briefly paraphrase my understanding of the attitudes which their lives reflected.

Adam and Eve: "Rather than permitting the Spirit of God to direct our lives through our obedience to Him, it would be better to direct our lives with our own minds and wills independently of God."

Cain: "It is better that I kill Abel rather than making my life and my sacrifices pleasing to God."

Samson: "It is not really necessary to avoid the company of evil women. I have consecrated my hair to God, so it is not really necessary to consecrate my sex life to him also." This resulted in the destruction of Samson by Delilah and the Philistines.

Abraham: "It is necessary for me to lie to the King and tell him that Sarah is my sister rather than my wife, in order to preserve my life and to avoid having those men kill me. I will trust in my own lie rather than to trust in God to protect me." Though the king discovered the lie, no harm came to Abraham.

Abraham demonstrated another attitude, which amounted to his spoken word to himself: "If God wants me to sacrifice Isaac, I can do so and still trust in Him to protect and provide for both Isaac and me." God spared Isaac, and Abraham demonstrated both to himself and to God that he was ready to become the great patriarch of the Jews.

Gideon: "God's promises and instructions are more reliable and powerful than the arrows, spears, and swords of the innumerable enemies before me." God revealed the truth of this attitude to Gideon.

Ruth: "I will remain loyal to my mother-in-law, and will do what is best in the eyes of God, rather than what seems more convenient at the moment." She became the great-grandmother of King David, and was thus placed in the line of Christ.

Queen Esther: "There may be enough power in the obedient, respectful attitude of a wife to reverse the plans and decrees of my husband, the king, to kill all of the Jews in his kingdom." She acted upon this assumption, and proved that it was correct.

Paul and Silas in prison: "We should praise God even though we have been beaten, jailed, and placed in the stocks." God responded to this attitude with an earthquake which opened the prison and freed them, converting the jailer and his family to Christianity.

Elisha to Captain Naaman (Naaman was the leper who came to Elisha for healing of his leprosy.): "Wash seven times in the Jordan River, and you will be healed." Naaman first felt, "There are rivers back home in Damascus. I didn't have to come all the way here to do this." But when Naaman, at the urging of his servants, proceeded to bathe seven times in the Jordan, the leprosy was healed. Chances are that there was not anything in the Jordan River that healed the leprosy. It was probably simple obedience to God, which seemed to be something totally new to Captain Naaman, that produced his healing.

Christ: "I come not to do my will, but the will of My Father in heaven." Result: all the miracles that He performed, and the salvation of all who accept Him.

Bibliography

1. Friedman, Meyer, And Rosenman, Ray H. **Type A Behavior And Your Heart.** New York: Alfred A. Knopf, 1974.
2. Simonton, O. Carl and Stephanie S. **Belief Systems And Management Of The Emotional Aspects Of Malignancy.** Journal Of Transpersonal Psychology 7:29-47, 1975.

Section Two:
Successful Christian Relationships
With Others

6

Christian Solutions To The Three Causes Of Depression

Depression! What's it all about? In 1 Kings 19:4, the Bible says that after the prophet Elijah had to flee to prevent Jezebel from killing him, he asked the Lord to take his life. In Jeremiah 20:14-18, Jeremiah cursed the day he was born when his preaching and prophesying were rejected and rewarded with imprisonment. Both men recovered from their depressions and continued to minister for the Lord. Depression is the most common emotional problem today. We all face depression at times in our lives. It is thus quite important that we have adequate means of understanding and coping with this problem.

I'd like to tell you about someone whom I was called upon to see, who demonstrated most of the ingredients that one sees in depression. This woman had been admitted to a hospital for abdominal pains. After the physical evaluation was completed, her physician asked me to see her, because it was apparent that there was no physical cause of her complaints. Depression was the problem, and it was causing both physical and emotional symptoms. I explored the cause of the depression in an interview with her. Many years previously, one of her children had drowned, and the depression began then. She was still getting herself admitted to hospitals as a result of the same depression over that loss, which had never been resolved. Her child had been of elementary school age at the time of her death. The swimming accident took place minutes after this mother had seen her daughter near the body of water in which the drowning took place. She had told her daughter to go inside the nearby house in which they were staying. A relative who was the same age as the daughter was visiting them. This child was not as obedient as the daughter was.

The woman described her daughter as an almost angelic little person who seemed to always do the right thing. It felt good merely to be around her. There was never a problem with her, and the mother had complete confidence in the daughter's obedience. She simply assumed that telling the daughter to go into the house would be met with obedience, and didn't double check. The other child then talked this daughter into going for a swim, and the daughter drowned. Ever since then, this woman had felt bitter toward God for having taken this child, and bitter toward the relative for having talked her child into this.

What do you say to someone who has lost a child? It is a very difficult problem, and I didn't know what to do except to go to the Scriptures and to ask in faith with her, "What did the Lord have in mind? Why did He take this child at that time? And what was she going to do about all the bitterness that she still felt toward the relative who had been involved in that situation?"

As the story unfolded, I learned that sometime after the child's drowning, this woman's husband began coming home drunk. He carried on so violently that it became necessary for her to separate from him with the ultimatum that he could come back when he rejected the alcohol. This cured the husband's alcoholism, and was followed by a reconciliation. Her husband had not taken a drink for many years at the time that I saw her.

Asking in faith what God had in mind, I thought about Isaiah 57:1, because of the father's alcoholism and its effects on the family. *"The righteous perisheth, and no man layeth it to heart; and merciful men are taken away, none considering that the righteous is taken away from the evil to come.''* It was apparent from everything that had been told to me about this child's life, that she had been removed just in time to prevent her from having to experience the evil that had afflicted that household for a long period of time.

I then explained to this bereaved mother that the Bible says that God wrote the names of those whom He is going to save in the Book of Life from the foundation of the world (Revelation 13:8). If God wrote our names in the Lamb's Book of Life before the creation of the earth, then He knew this woman before she was born. He knew her child before the child was born. Knowing all that, God could have given this woman any child that He wanted to give her. But He gave her **this** child, whose appointed time to die (Ecclesiastes 3:1-2) was at an early age. This mother had entered into despair when the child drowned. This resulted in her becoming a born-again Christian a few years later. It also resulted in her leading her husband to be nearly ready to accept Christ. Though he had not accepted the Lord yet, she was quite confident that it was going to happen soon because of the spiritual growth he had recently begun to manifest.

In a combined effort to get her mind off her loss and to compensate for it, she had become involved in civic activities on behalf of children. She had accomplished some extremely important work for the benefit of children in need, that even politicians had tried unsuccessfully to do. It was apparent that a great deal of good had come about through the death of this daughter. This woman also had a younger daughter who had witnessed the drowning as well as the events preceding it. It was apparent that this child had received a very important lesson regarding the benefit of obedience to parental authority. Obedience to parental authority is extremely important, because a person who is rebellious toward a parent is rebellious to God, and ruins his life very easily. There were even more aspects to this case in which one could see the perfection of God's work in all of these lives.

In reviewing these scriptural truths with this woman, I saw

her depression lifting, as she looked in faith at what God had already done in the lives of herself and her family through the death of that child. Her husband had taken that death in a different way. When she later separated from him with the ultimatum, "You must give up your alcoholism, and you can come back when you do," it seemed much more likely that he would choose to come back to that family, because his need for the family had been increased as a result of the loss of that child. One could go on and on, seeing what God was probably doing through the death of that child, by reviewing it in faith.

The Three Causes Of Depression

Depression is usually caused by one of three things: bitterness towards God, bitterness toward another person, or bitterness toward oneself. When we experience bitterness towards anyone, that bitterness gets turned back upon ourselves in the form of depression. In Matthew 22, Verses 37-40, *"Jesus said unto him, Thou shalt love the Lord thy God with all thy heart, and with all thy soul, and with all thy mind. 38 - This is the first and great commandment. 39 - And the second is like unto it, Thou shalt love thy neighbour as thyself. 40 - On these two commandments hang all the law and the prophets."* Depression is thus usually caused by a violation of these two great commandments, because bitterness toward God, a neighbor, or yourself is a violation of one of them.

The concept that bitterness becomes depression is indicated in various ways in the Scriptures. In Matthew 6:22-23, the Bible says, *"The light of the body is the eye: if therefore thine eye be single, thy whole body shall be full of light. 23 - But if thine eye be evil, thy whole body shall be full of darkness. If therefore the light that is in thee be darkness, how great is that darkness!"* One thing being taught here is that we become whatever we focus our thoughts upon. Depression is mentally associated with darkness. Depressed people who paint often use a predominance of black. Whenever the Bible speaks of darkness, it is also speaking of the dominion of Satan, which is also at work with any type of emotional illness. The Second Epistle of Paul to Timothy, 1:7 teaches, *"For God hath not given us the spirit of fear, but of power, and of love, and of a sound mind."*

In Luke, 6:38, Christ says, *"Give, and it shall be given unto you; good measure, pressed down, and shaken together, and running over, shall men give into your bosom. For with the same measure that ye mete withal it shall be measured to you again."* If you respond to others with bitterness, it is returned to you. In John 8:34, *"Jesus answered them, Verily, verily, I say unto you, Whosoever committeth sin is the servant of sin."* Thus, if we commit our lives to bitterness, we become the victims of it. Ephesians 4:26-27 says, *"Be ye angry, and sin not; let not the sun go down upon your wrath: 27 - Neither give place to the devil."* The statement, "neither give place to the devil," suggests that by nurturing wrath, the destructive effects of the resulting depression manifest the work of the devil.

Bitterness Toward God:
The First Cause Of Depression

Why do people become bitter toward God? It may be because of loss of health, finances, or the loss of an important relationship. Perhaps a spouse, or a child, or a parent has died. Someone may have caused an injury somehow, and God let it happen. In any depression, one may experience bitterness toward God for letting the hurtful event occur. The person asks, "Why me? Why did God let this happen to me?" Whenever that question is asked outside of faith, one then injects lies into the mind, creating additonal problems. The lies are attitudes such as the following. "I'm smarter than God." "God doesn't love me." "God doesn't have the power to help me." "God doesn't have the wisdom to know what I need." "God won't give me what I want, so He's not there."

101

Phillipians 4:19 says, *"But my God shall supply all your need according to his riches in glory by Christ Jesus."* The Bible promises here that God will give us what we need, not everything we **want**. I once heard a preacher on the radio preaching on this verse. He said that the problem with most people is that their "wanters" were a lot bigger than their "needers." That's true. Not only is the magnitude of the things that we want sometimes much more than we need, but the direction and nature of what we want are often erroneous. We can often look back upon our past wants and realize how totally different was what we desired from what God was trying to provide us.

Eight Solutions To Bitterness Toward God

Solution Number One:
Recognizing That God Is Infinitely Wiser
Than We Are Prevents Depression

God gives to us and protects us based on His perfect wisdom for our lives. It is easy for us to forget that God's wisdom is infinitely greater than ours. One solution to bitterness toward God is realizing that God is trying to provide what each of us needs in His unlimited wisdom, and that is often very different from what we want, because we don't have His knowledge of the future regarding our lives.

Solution Number Two:
Recognizing God's Character Construction
In Us Heals Depression

Another question that is very helpful in dealing with bitterness towards God is, "What is God trying to build in my life through this experience?" When you ask that in faith, you will always get the answer. If you will pray in that way, asking God to reveal to you what He is trying to build in your life, while assuming that whatever He does is truly the best

102

thing for your life, you will rapidly get some very important answers.

Solution Number Three:
Applying God's Promises To Life
Situations Heals Depression.

The Bible tells us that man does not live by bread alone, but by every word that proceeds out of the mouth of the Lord (Deuteronomy 8:3, Matthew 4:4). One of the things that this means is that there is a promise of God in the Bible to cover every important mental, verbal, and physical human activity. Another solution to bitterness towards God, or towards anyone else, is to become familiar with the promises in the Bible that pertain to the situation in which we find ourselves. By doing that, we can often discover that something we have done in the past guaranteed the outcome that we have now experienced. The promises are always, "If you do such and such, God will do thus and so." The Bible repetitively promises peace, joy, and fruitfulness for following the teachings of Christ, and despair for rejecting His protective instructions for living. If we are in a situation in which unpleasant occurrences have befallen us, then we can often find those promises whose conditions we fulfilled to bring them about. We can then reject whatever we may have been doing that has been bringing about those undesirable consequences. That mental, verbal, or physical behavior can then be replaced with new attitudes or behavior which would put us in a position to fulfill the desirable promises. We can thus stop fulfilling the conditions of those promises of despair, and begin fulfilling the conditions of those promises of peace, joy, and fruitfulness. We will always get exactly what is promised in the Scriptures. Observing the fulfillment of the promises of God is one of the most amazing things that I have ever experienced. God's promises are kept in 100% of the cases in lives today, just as they were thousands of years ago.

A middle aged man whom I counselled had been bitter nearly all of his life. The primary cause of his depression was that when he was in elementary school, his parents rejected him from their household and sent him to live in the household of a relative. He had been hating his parents all of those decades, and had become so depressed that he could no longer work. He had become mentally disabled. It was all that he could do to keep from committing suicide. In reviewing his life with him, it was apparent that he had failed to fully look at the details of what had happened. This was initially a situation in which his father had forsaken him due to the father's chronic depression and character defects. Not long after he was removed from the parental home, both of his parents died. He had thus become a member of the category of the **fatherless**. In many places in the Bible, God promises to be a special protector of the fatherless, whether the father has died or whether the father has forsaken the child.[3] It has been very interesting to me to review the lives of fatherless people who have matured, and to look at how God has kept his promises to those people. It doesn't matter that the individual doesn't know that these promises exist. God knows that He promised it, and He cannot lie or break a promise (Numbers 23:19).

This man had been provided with two foster parents who treated him better in every way than his parents had: in their characters, in their interest in him, and in their love for him. There was no question that his life had turned out far better as a result of his foster parents' influence on him.

Later in his therapy, he realized that his mother died of cancer only several months after this family had "rejected" him from their home. No doubt, his mother knew that she was dying of cancer when this was done. His parents had simply lied to him. Rather than being told the truth, he was told that there wasn't enough space in the house for him, so he had to live with someone else. His mother was probably trying to protect him from the knowledge that she was going to die. Though she erred in lying to him, the whole thing had been an exercise in protecting him and providing for him both by his mother and by God. Yet, he had been so bitter about this for so long, that he had ruined his life.

Solution Number Four:
Thankfulness Prevents Depression

Another way of dealing with bitterness toward God is found in Romans 8:28, *"And we know that all things work together for good to them that love God, to them who are the called according to his purpose."* That can be combined with 1 Thessalonians 5:18, *"In everything give thanks: for this is the will of God in Christ Jesus concerning you."*

This is the cornerstone of the Christian life: to recognize the love and the power of God to provide exactly what we need, so long as we are following His laws and teachings. Thanking God for what He is going to do through any stressful, depressing situation that we face, will do a great deal to eliminate depression. It is impossible to be both thankful and depressed at the same time. Thankfulness is the opposite of self pity.

Solution Number Five:
Rejecting Self Pity Prevents Depression

Another thing that can be done to counteract depression that is caused by bitterness toward God or toward anyone else, is to reject self pity. Through self pity, one will create depression as well as greatly magnify an existing depression. A person engaged in self pity thinks, "Poor me. Look how much I'm suffering. Look at what awful things happen to me. Why does it always have to happen to me? Why doesn't God care more about me? Why doesn't anyone love me?" In this manner, one can quickly work himself up from a minor depression to an overwhelming one. Tim LeHaye covers this subject well in his popular book, **How To Win Over Depression.**[1]

Solution Number Six:
The Decision To Demonstrate Courage
Prevents Depression

Depression caused by bitterness toward God or by a difficult situation can be overcome by a decision to demonstrate courage. Where there is depression there is usually fear. Fear of what's going to happen to me. Fear of what's going to happen if what I want doesn't take place. Fear of what's going to happen if the undesirable situation that I'm worried about does come about. Fear of what's going to happen if the tribulation that I'm experiencing doesn't end as soon as I would like. Nothing is more poisonous to the human mind than fear. God commands us to demonstrate courage rather than fear throughout the Bible.[2] The Book of Revelations 21:7-8 goes even further:

"7 - He that overcometh shall inherit all things; and I will be his God, and he shall be my son.
"8 - But the fearful and unbelieving, and the abominable, and murderers, and whoremongers, and sorcerors, and idolators, and all liars, shall have their part in the lake which burneth with fire and brimstone: which is the second death."

God apparently hates fear. The reason for this is probably that when one makes a decision to demonstrate fear, fear then has dominion over him. At that point, there is no limit to what he might do to avoid fear. Satan then has his way in that life. King David feared discovery of his adultery with Bathsheba. He responded by arranging the murder of her husband and then marrying her. All this was to conceal the fact that she had become pregnant by David. The things one will do in response to fear are disastrous.

On the other hand, if you make a decision that you are going to **demonstrate** courage, no matter what you **feel,** and no matter what you face, then you eventually **feel** courage.

106

You begin acting and living on courage rather than acting and living on fear. It is as if there were a see-saw in the mind with fear on one side of it, and courage on the other. Whenever you make a decision that you are going to **act** in response to fear, the fear end of the see-saw comes up, and the courage goes down. The next thing you know, you can't see courage within you. Consequently, even if you are afraid, make a simple decision: "I am going to demonstrate courage, no matter what I feel, no matter what I face. Even if I were to be about to die, I could demonstrate courage. Even if I were paralyzed from the neck down, I could demonstrate courage." When you make that kind of decision, courage comes up in the mind, and fear goes down and progressively diminishes. Every time you make the decision to demonstrate courage, every time that you act upon the decision to demonstrate courage, fear continues to dissipate, until soon it is totally gone.

Solution Number Seven:
Placing Money In Proper Perspective
Prevents Depression

When depressed because of bitterness toward God or toward anyone else in situations of financial difficulty, tell yourself, "It's only money." Many unrealistic values are usually attached to money. To many people, money is an index of self worth. This is obviously a false value. Attila the Hun and Adolph Hitler were very wealthy people. Yet historically, most people have not held them in high esteem. The statement, "It's only money," serves to reject the negative suggestions usually attached to money. False values attached to money are a special problem to people who experienced extreme poverty in childhood. Such individuals were usually embarrassed as children because their peers were better dressed and had many basic things that they lacked. They often experienced teasing and ridicule for not having shoes or not having better clothes. The message of such teasing is, "I'm a better person than you are because I have more material things." Such an individual who suddenly loses money or enters financial stress in adult life usually re-experiences childhood feelings of, "I'm not as good as I should be, because I don't have more money." Rejecting such lies heals depression. The truth is, "It's only money."

Solution Number Eight:
Placing Time In Proper Perspective
Heals Depression

If you are depressed about some situation, tell yourself, "It will pass." Those are three very important words, no matter what you face, chances are that it **will** pass. Even if you had a permanent loss, your grief about that loss will pass. You will recover from it, so long as you don't mentally stop yourself from recovering by means of chronic bitterness and depression.

Whenever a person finds himself in a stressful situation, he often loses perspective of the fact that the situation usually represents a small segment of his life span. It is helpful to think of past stressful situations which seemed as though they would never end, but which did pass. Subsequently, such past events usually seem much more brief when we look back on them.

Bitterness Towards Others:
The Second Cause Of Depression

The next major cause of depression is bitterness towards others, whoever the others may be. You could put them in the category of your "neighbors." Whenever one is suffering from a depression based on bitterness toward someone else, he is inevitably telling himself lies. Lies such as, "It is better to be bitter than to forgive as Christ taught us to do." Lies such as, "If I stay bitter long enough, that person is somehow going to pay for what he has done to me." Depression is also caused by lies such as, "If my parents continue to hurt me, it will be necessary for me to have a nervous breakdown." Lies such as, "The best way for me to respond to the childhood rejection that I received from my parents is to become something that they will be ashamed of." Lies such as, "If I forgive my parents for their childhood rejection or abuse of me, I will do **them** a favor and not myself." Rejecting such lies makes forgiveness and healing of depression possible. Chronic depression which begins in childhood and continues in adult life is usually caused by bitterness towards parents for rejection. Depression of adult onset is usually caused by bitterness toward someone else, such as a boss, or a spouse, or a friend.

Seven Solutions To Bitterness Toward Others

Solution Number One:
Communication Can Prevent Depression

One solution to depression caused by bitterness toward a person who has hurt you, or is hurting you, is to go to that person and tell him, "What you are doing is hurting me, and it would mean a lot to me if you would stop that." Most people are afraid to do this, because they imagine that it would cause them to lose that relationship. This is exactly the opposite of what usually happens. When you do that, it is likely to enhance that relationship. The other person will usually begin thinking more highly of you. He realizes that you're being honest with him, and that you care enough about that relationship and about him to try to improve it. The usual outcome is an important improvement in the relationship. Two people begin feeling much closer if they feel free to honestly express their feelings to each other.

On the other hand, if that person refuses to change his behavior, it may then become necessary for you to limit the amount of time that you spend with him, or to totally avoid him. Many Scriptures tell us these very things. In Matthew

18:15-17, Christ teaches His disciples, *"Moreover if thy brother shall trespass against thee, go and tell him his fault between him and thee alone: if he shall hear thee, thou hast gained thy brother. 16 - But if he will not hear thee, then take with thee one or two more, that in the mouth of two or three witnesses every word may be established. 17 - And if he shall neglect to hear them, tell it unto the church: but if he neglect to hear the church, let him be unto thee as an heathen man and a publican."* Publicans were tax collectors. Everyone despised them because they were financially abusing people so badly in those days. These Scriptures provide an excellent prescription for responding to someone who is hurting you. The instruction to take one or two others to an offending brother provides some protection against error. Maybe you are angry with someone else because of **your** problem. Maybe **you** are misinterpreting reality. Maybe **you** have an emotional hang-up which is really causing the whole problem, and you are blaming it on the other person. If you will take another observer with you to review the situation, you will have an objective observer to help redirect you if you're the culprit, or if you're involved in a misunderstanding. If it is your Christian brother who is being inappropriate, that objective observer may redirect him. Here in the gospel we see a built-in protection from people lying to themselves in their relationships and not realizing it.

Solution Number Two:
Limiting Or Avoiding The Company Of
Malicious People Can Prevent Depression

Though it is rare, some people have evil parents who have so placed themselves under the dominion of evil, that the best thing their grown children can do is to limit the amount of time that they spend with them. Such parents may constantly criticize or cut down everything that their children and anyone else say or do. They are full of hatred. Some find that they have to protect themselves from spending too much time

110

in the presence of such a parent in order to avoid having "nervous breakdowns." I have seen a number of people enter asylums following week long visits from parents who would have to be classified as basically evil people. I have seen people who were staying constantly depressed because they were mentally holding on to bitterness by constantly reviewing all of the awful things that their parents did to them during childhood. Some parents in fact do hateful and painful things to their children. Many adults who had such childhood relationships with parents become depressed because of mis-interpretations of Scriptures. The Scriptures say, "**Honour** thy father and thy mother" (Exodus 20:12), rather than saying, "Love thy father and thy mother." Many adults feel that if they don't have a deep love for such a rejecting, unlikeable parent, this is a sin. They feel that they must justify not having a deep love for that parent or not spending a great deal of time with that parent, by constantly reviewing all of the awful things that ever happened to them at the hands of that parent. This produces chronic re-living of the childhood pain, and becomes self pity, which causes depression. Correcting such a mis-interpretation of Scriptures is very helpful in this type of situation.

Christ made it clear when He instructed His disciples to go out and preach that they were not to minister to everyone, and were not to associate with everyone. In Matthew 7:6, Christ taught, *"Give not that which is holy unto the dogs, neither cast ye your pearls before swine, lest they trample them under their feet, and turn again and rend you."* Christ also instructed His disciples in the following verses of Matthew, Chapter Ten.

> *"5 - These twelve Jesus sent forth, and commanded them, saying, Go not into the way of the Gentiles, and into any city of the Samaritans enter ye not."*
> *"11 - And into whatsoever city or town ye shall enter, enquire who in it is worthy; and there abide till ye go thence.*

111

"12 - And when ye come into an house, salute it.

"13 - And if the house be worthy, let your peace come upon it: but if it be not worthy, let your peace return to you.

"14 - And whosoever shall not receive you, nor hear your words, when ye depart out of that house or city, shake off the dust of your feet.

"16 - Behold, I send you forth as sheep in the midst of wolves: be ye therefore wise as serpents, and harmless as doves."

Christ makes it clear that we must be careful with whom we associate. We've got to be as wise as the serpent or his representatives, or else we'll be torn up by people who are under the dominion of satanic influence. If it becomes realistically necessary to avoid a person in order to avoid being damaged by him, then this is obviously consistent with what Christ taught His disciples and thus taught us. We are His disciples today, if we are Christians, and those principles which He taught His disciples then, apply to us now.

Solution Number Three:
Looking for God's Love and Wisdom During
Tribulation Prevents Depression

What if your neighbor is sinning against you, and you can't stop it? Maybe it's your spouse. What if a boss is doing disrespectful or harmful things to you, and you have a year or two left to retirement? Perhaps you've been working nineteen of the twenty years that would qualify you for retirement benefits, and you don't want to give up the job. You've got to stay there and let the boss sin against you in order to obtain your retirement. There are many situations in which someone may sin against us, and we can't immediately free ourselves from those situations. Two concepts are needed to address being sinned against in an unchangeable situation. The first is to ask the question, "What character strengths is God trying to build in me by subjecting me to this situation with this person at this time? God knows who I am, and He knows who this other person is. He knew us before we were even born (Rev. 17:8, 13:8). He knew that this would happen, and He put me into this situation and locked me into it for a time. What is He trying to build in me, based on His love, wisdom, and knowledge of me?'' Whenever I have asked that question in faith regarding my life or that of someone I have counselled, I have always received important, useful answers. The second concept needed for such unchangeable situations is presented below.

Solution Number Four:
Recognizing God's Justice Prevents Depression

The next concept that we need to apply when someone is sinning against us, and we can't stop it, is the spiritual truth that no sin goes unpunished. The absence of this concept is a real weakness in the average Christian's life. For some reason, the average Christian does not believe that sins will get punished. Many believe that if someone sins against them, the antagonist can merely ask God for forgiveness and he will get away with it. People who believe this are reluctant to forgive, because they feel that the offending party will go unpunished for the offense. The New Testament teaches that God forgives us, and that He won't cast us into hell if we repent for our sins and confess them. But He will punish us. The punishment will be based on his love and wisdom, and through it, He will reveal Himself. He will use that punishment to build character in us and to turn our lives around toward Him. Galatians, 6:7 tells us, *"Be not deceived; God is not mocked; for whatsoever a man soweth, that shall he also reap."* In Matthew 26:52, Christ instructs Peter (See John 18:10) when he cut off the ear of one of the high priest's servants who came to apprehend Christ. *"Then said Jesus unto him, Put up again thy sword into his place: for all they that take the sword shall perish with the sword."*

113

Revelation 13:10 teaches, *"He that leadeth into captivity shall go into captivity: he that killeth with the sword must be killed with the sword. Here is the patience and the faith of the saints."* Right there, the Bible is teaching that you can have patience and can keep your faith, because no matter what anyone does to you, you can know that he will be properly punished for it.

Solution Number Five:
Avoiding Unrealistic Responsibility For Being
Rejected Prevents Depression

If someone is hurting you and you're depressed about it, it is important to make certain that you are not feeling like a bad person merely because that person is rejecting you. Many people have experienced some parental rejection in childhood. When they were children, they assumed that their parents were always right. They concluded in childhood that if their parents rejected them, they must have been bad, unloveable children. They go through life feeling like they are bad people, because their parents rejected them. Children don't normally think of a parent as having emotional problems or character defects. In a child's mind, whatever a parent does is right: so if a parent abuses a child, it means that the child is just no good; he deserves to be treated that way. Later, when someone is hurting him in adult life, he starts to feel like a bad, worthless person all over again. All of this mental pain is based on that series of lies that one has told himself from childhood. Identifying those lies and replacing them with truth frees one from the bondage of that emotional pain.

Solution Number Six:
Taking Dominion Over Satan Can
Prevent Depression

Another thing that can be done in dealing with bitterness toward God, or bitterness toward anyone else, is to take dominion over Satan. If someone is actively doing something harmful to you, you are not merely dealing with that individual. He has probably placed himself under the influence of satanic dominion. I realize that many people don't believe in the devil. That position may make one especially vulnerable, because no enemy is more powerful than one whose presence is not even recognized. There is no limit to the amount of havoc that such an enemy can create in one's life.

The Bible tells us that we do not struggle against mere flesh and blood, but against powers that are under the dominion of Satan. Ephesians, 6:12 tells us, *"For we wrestle not against flesh and blood, but against principalities, against powers, against the rulers of the darkness of this world, against spiritual wickedness in high places."* Those are different levels or ranks in the hierarchy of Satan's army of demons. You may find yourself in a situation in which someone else is huring or damaging you. If you have no influence over that person, you can take dominion over the satanic power to which that person is responding.

Many people don't realize that God has given Christians dominion over the devil. In The First Epistle of John, 4:4, the Bible promises, *". . . Greater is he that is in you, than he that is in the world."* In Luke 10:19, Christ says, *"Behold, I give unto you the power to tread on serpents and scorpions, and over all the power of the enemy; and nothing shall by any means hurt you."*

When I attended dinner at my twenty year high school graduation class reunion, I was sitting two places away from a couple who was chain smoking. The woman was smoking cigarettes, and the man was smoking cigarellos. When a non-smoker who hasn't lost the sense of smell, tries to eat dinner with smoke blowing into his face, all he tastes and smells is the smoke. I am allergic to cigarette smoke, anyway. Most people are, even smokers. That's why they often develop chronic sinusitis and chronic bronchitis. I wanted to enjoy my dinner, so I simply recalled those scriptural promises. I said to myself, "These people are being very inconsiderate. They know that people don't like to eat cigarette smoke for dinner, and here they are chain smoking." Their smoking had proceeded continually for approximately half an hour. No empty seats were available, so it was impossible to escape the cigarette smoke by moving to another location.

At that point, I decided to take dominion over Satan. I didn't speak out loud, only mentally. Satan knows our thoughts, just as God knows our thoughts (Job 1:9-12, 2:5-6). He looks in our hearts, just as God does, and he can gain dominion over us through our minds. So I said, "I command in the name of Jesus Christ that Satan be bound and removed from those two people and from this entire situation, right now." From that moment, neither of these two people smoked again, for the remainder of that function, though we were at that table for another hour.

God has already given us promises of dominion over Satan, but it is up to us to utilize that dominion. Many Christians pray to God to protect them from Satan while failing to use that dominion which He has already given them. This may be compared to a person in normal health who wishes to leave a room. Rather than getting up out of his seat and walking out, he begins praying to God to lift him up and carry him out of the room. That prayer probably wouldn't be answered. God would probably look down and say, "Look at this fellow, praying for Me to do what I have already given him the ability to do." Likewise, we must use the dominion that God has already given us over Satan.

Solution Number Seven:
Rejecting Bitterness Toward Others
Prevents Depression

Past events can no longer hurt us. Rather, it is usually our bitterness about those events which produces emotional pain or despair. Forgiveness can release us from the bonds of bitterness that connect us to the pain of past experiences or to

116

the pain associated with people who hurt us in the past. When depressed because someone hurt you, it is quite helpful to visualize ropes of bitterness connecting you with every person and situation through which you have been hurt. Whether it is your parent, your spouse, a friend, anyone, just close your eyes and visualize those ropes of bitterness connecting you with them. You'll find that those ropes seem real. Ropes of emotion mentally bind you to situations and persons toward whom you are bitter. Visualize yourself taking a large sword in your hands, and cutting through every one of those ropes of bitterness. You will immediately release yourself from that depression.

A daily prayer asking God to cleanse your heart of all bitterness and hatred is also very helpful in these situations.

A daily prayer asking God to heal your painful memories is likewise helpful.

Bitterness Toward Oneself:
The Third Cause of Depression

The last category of depression is caused by bitterness toward oneself. This is usually the result of unforgiveness of oneself for past sins. During my practice of psychiatry, I have learned the intimate details of the personal lives of many people in all walks of life. One of the most impressive lessons I have learned from this is that every person has experienced something in his life that would make him terribly ashamed if it were suddenly projected on a movie screen before a large audience. This seems to be one thing that the Bible is referring to when it teaches in Romans 3:23, *"For all have sinned, and come short of the glory of God."*

Three Solutions To Bitterness Toward Oneself

Solution Number One:
Accepting God's Forgiveness Heals Depression

The First Epistle of John, 1:8-10, teaches: *"If we say that we have no sin, we deceive ourselves, and the truth is not in us. 9 - If we confess our sins, he is faithful and just to forgive us our sins, and to cleanse us from all unrighteousness. 10 - If we say that we have not sinned, we make him a liar, and his word is not in us."*

The Bible is telling us that everyone of us at times sins. We all have reason to be ashamed of ourselves. We're all "in the same boat." But God promises that if we confess our sins, He is faithful to forgive us. If anyone is feeling that he is a bad, no-good person, and that God is not forgiving him for confessed sin, it is important to look at these Scriptures. Denying that God has forgiven you is like trying to make a liar of God, because He has promised in writing that He will forgive any confessed sin. Be certain that what you say is identical to what God says in this regard.

Solution Number Two:
Using The Past To Build Character, Humility, And Love Of God Heals Depression

If you are bitter toward yourself for something you have done in the past, ask yourself, "What is God trying to build in me through my past sins?" Moses killed an Egyptian when he was forty years old. By the time he was eighty, the Bible says that he was the humblest man on earth (Numbers 12:3). That's the man that God picked to go and lead the Jews out of Israel. No doubt, the death of that Egyptian had changed Moses and humbled him. Whenever he looked back to that event, he must have realized what he would be if he functioned only by his own will. This would have inevitably made him conscious of the great need for the Lord to lead him in his life. Paul was one of the greatest of Christians in terms of what he did to build the church. He persecuted the Christians extensively before his conversion. In 1 Corinthians 15:9-10, Paul says, *"For I am the least of the apostles, that am not meet to be called an apostle, because I persecuted the church of God. 10 - But by the grace of God I am what I am:*

*and his grace which was bestowed upon me was not in vain;
but I laboured more abundantly than they all: yet not I, but
the grace of God which was with me.''*

Paul's past caused him to be humble toward the Lord. As a
result, God chose to work in great ways through him. In Luke
Chapter Seven, the Pharisee mentally rebuked Christ for
permitting the sinful woman to wash His feet with her tears,
dry them with her hair, and annoint them. Christ responded
with a parable of two debtors whose debts were cancelled by a
creditor. The debtor who owed most, loved the creditor
more. Christ concluded in Verse 47, *"Wherefore I say unto
thee, Her sins, which are many, are forgiven; for she loved
much: but to whom little is forgiven, the same loveth little.''*
This is an astounding spiritual truth! Christ taught here that
those who love Him most are those whose past confessed sins
have been the greatest. The shame and ugliness of past sin
should thus be replaced with an awareness of deeper love for
God, who forgives us. The message is clear. We should not
wallow around in self contempt for past sins. Instead, we
should permit our love of God to fill our awareness and
emanate to those around us.

Solution Number Three:
The Plan Of Salvation Heals Depression

A third and last thing that you can do if you are bitter
towards yourself and depressed because of something in the
past, is to apply the plan of salvation. You may have been
ashamed of past wrongful financial dealings, or divorce, or
fornication, or adultery, or an abortion. Perhaps you know
that one of your grown children was mentally damaged as a
result of your own character defects during his childhood. No
matter what it is, you can use the plan of salvation to handle
it in this way. Simply tell yourself, "Christ died for my sins.
The Bible says that the wages of sin is death. Though I
deserve the death penalty, I accept that Christ died in my
place. Consequently, I don't have to physically die. Instead, I

will die to my self will. When Christ died in my place, He ransomed me from death. He bought me with his blood, so He consequently owns me now. From now on, I will die to my self will. My life and actions will be determined by His will, His laws, His teachings, His word. I will accept Christ's blood as my ransom, and I now belong to Him." To that kind of attitude, Christ says in Revelation 3:20, *"Behold, I stand at the door, and knock: if any man hear my voice, and open the door, I will come in to him, and will sup with him, and he with me."* In other words, if you will give your life to Christ, He will give His life to you!

Bibliography

1. LeHaye, Tim. **How To Win Over Depression.** Grand Rapids, Michigan: Zondervan Publishing House, 1974.
2. Scriptural references for courage:
   Deuteronomy 31:6, 31:8, 31:23
   Isaiah 43:1, 43:5, 44:8
   Joshua 1:5-6, 1:9, 8:1
   1 Chronicles 22:13
   Zechariah 8:9, 8:13
   John 14:27
   Revelation 21:7-8
3. Scriptural references in which God promises that He will be the Father to the fatherless and the protector of widows.
   Exodus 22:22-24
   Deuteronomy 10:18; 14:28-29; 16:11,14; 24:17-22; 26:12-13; 27:19
   Psalms 10:14; 10:17-18
   Psalms 27:10 *"When my father and my mother forsake me, then the Lord will take me up."*
   Psalms 68:5; 82:3
   Proverbs 23:10-11
   Isaiah 1:17; 1:23-24; 10:1-2
   Jeremiah 5:28-29; 7:6-7; 22:3; 49:11
   Hoseah 14:3-5
   Malachi 3:5
   James 1:27

7

Successful Christian Response
To Being Sinned Against

Being sinned against! How do you cope with it without either getting depressed or violating Christ's teachings? The Bible tells us that we are all sinners (Romans 3:23, 1 John 1:8-10). It doesn't take long in relationships to discover that sooner or later people are likely to somehow sin against us, and we against them. We must therefore have in readiness successful Christian responses to those who sin against us. We are certain to need them.

A middle aged man had suffered from chronic and recurrent depression, periodic loss of touch with reality, and episodes of alcoholism. I put a fancy label on his condition: **Manic depressive psychosis.** The diagnosis was correct, but this label implies a grim outlook, with little hope of cure. Prior to my treating this man, there had often seemed to be little that could be done to treat this disorder, except to prescribe medication. Many different medications had been used in this case. Each time a new medication was tried, it would produce temporary improvement which would be followed shortly by despair. After many disappointments with medications, I told him, "You know, it is fairly obvious that the Lord is stopping you and me from getting you well with pills. It may be that there is something in your life that He wants changed. You have been remaining sick, and I think it is because something that we are not seeing has got to be changed." We then agreed to conduct a rapid analysis of his problems. This revealed that his past drunkenness, his depression, and his psychotic breaks had all been caused by bitterness towards his father from childhood. His father had rejected him severely. During the formative years of this man's childhood, his father had made it clear that to him, this son wasn't worth any time, attention, or affection. Here he was decades later, in a seemingly hopeless condition which he couldn't resolve, except by considering suicide so strongly that he had admitted himself to a hospital. I asked him, "Why don't you simply forgive your father? Don't you see that it is your refusal to forgive that has been causing all these problems?" "No!" He refused to consider forgiving his father. "Why not?" "Doc, I feel that if I forgive my Daddy, he will get away with all the dirty, rotten things he did to me throughout my childhood." I replied, "Don't you know that the Lord has promised not to let any sin go unpunished, and your father couldn't get away with all that? The Lord took care of that in His ways." But he wouldn't forgive. He said, "No. My father had a good life, and though he died several years ago, he did not get punished for all the things he did to me." I said, "Well, I don't know any more about your father's life than what you are telling me, but I know what God has promised. I know that your father somehow got punished for his sins. I know that if you knew everything about your father's life and told me everything about his life, then we would see what happened in this regard. I'd like you to think about this, because this is very important to you." That was the end of that session.

The next day I returned to see him in the hospital. He said, "You know, Doc, since our session yesterday, I have remembered that my father was senile the last several years of his life. During that time, he was obsessed by the fear that somebody was going to get him back for something wrong that he had done to them, but he didn't know what it was. This went on for years." I asked, "Why didn't you tell me that yesterday?" "Well, I've always been afraid that I would end up just like him, and I didn't want to remember that." I showed him some more of God's promises, such as Luke 6:46-49, which promises that if we follow all of Christ's teachings, then our lives and our personalities will look like a house built on stone when the flood waters of life come up against it. And if we reject Christ's teachings, when the flood waters of life come up against us, then our lives and our personalities will look like a house built on mud and will be ruined. I told him that he had simply been making himself heir to the wrong set of Christ's promises. If he wanted to avoid what happened to his father, he simply needed to reverse some of the things that he had been doing. I couldn't promise what was going to happen to him, because I didn't know. All I could tell him was what Christ had promised, and that whenever I look at lives, I see the promises of Christ being fulfilled in every life, and never contradicted. They have to be kept, or Christ would become a liar. He is not going to be a liar for anybody's sins.

We must not gloat when someone else gets punished, because that involves a spirit of vengence. We must avoid telling ourselves, "Aha! I am so glad that evil has befallen that person." But we do need to know that it is safe to place things in God's hands when we are being sinned against. We need to know that God isn't blind, He is not uncaring, and He is not powerless. He knows what is happening to us, and He could stop such events anytime that He wishes, even before they ever begin. If He doesn't stop them before they begin, it is because He plans to use those experiences to somehow build our lives the way He knows our lives need to become for our own benefit.

Three important points must be remembered whenever we face the problem of someone sinning against us and hurting us. The first concept is that God promises throughout both Testaments that no sin goes unpunished. The second concept is that God's punishment of sin is often not immediate, but is usually delayed. The third concept is that the tribulation we experience when someone sins against us is often used by God to build character in us.

No Sin Goes Unpunished

The first principle, that no sin goes unpunished, is taught by Scriptures throughout both Testaments. God promises forgiveness of confessed sin (1 John 1:9), and He will not send us to hell for it. He modifies the punishment according to His wisdom and love, but punishment must occur. It is very important that we understand this in contending with our own sin tendencies as well as those who sin against us. Revelations, Chapter 13, Verse 10, tells us, *"He that leadeth into captivity shall go into captivity: he that killeth with the sword must be killed with the sword. Here is the patience and the faith of the saints."* Whenever the Bible refers to the saints, it is talking about the members of Christ's church, all Christians. God's promise to punish every sin is one basis for our forgiving others, though this is not the only basis. Another reason for forgiveness is that we are to love other people and see them as humans afflicted with sin tendencies, as we ourselves are. The Bible's statement, "Here is the patience and the faith of the Saints," implies that Christians can trust God's justice. It would seem quite impossible for God to have a perfect system of justice without principles such as this with which to run the Universe. Galatians 6:7 teaches, *"Be not deceived; God is not mocked: for whatsoever a man soweth, that shall he also reap."* This indicates that God will not be made a fool over anyone's sins. In 2 Thessalonians 1:6, Paul writes, *"Seeing it is a righteous thing with God to recompense tribulation to them that trouble you."* The Bible is promising that if somebody troubles you, God will repay them with trouble.

We can see the principle that no sin goes unpunished illustrated in the life of Paul. Paul spent a great deal of time persecuting Christians prior to his conversion. He then underwent an enormous amount of persecution in his own Christian ministry after his conversion. The tribulations which Paul endured were the very things that he had previously inflicted upon the Christians. Though God had to punish Paul for those sins, He used those punishing experiences for the glorification of God, and even for the glorification of Paul. Paul is greatly admired for his courageous endurance of the beatings, stoning, and imprisonments which he experienced during his ministry. In the 9th Chapter of Acts, we are told about Paul's conversion when Christ appeared to him on the road to Damascus. He was given temporary blindness, and was instructed to go on to the city. There he was to go to a particular house. Christ directed another Christian named Ananias to go and lay hands on Paul, at which time his sight would be restored. This was to be a confirmation to Paul that it was Christ directing his experiences. When Christ appeared to Ananias to communicate his part in this, Ananias basically objected (Verses 13 and 14) that Paul had not only been persecuting Christians in Jerusalem, but he had even come to Damascus for the same purpose. How shocked Ananias must have been that Christ now wanted him to participate in Paul's healing! Christ replied to Ananias, in Acts 9:16, *"For I will show him (Paul) how great things he must suffer for my name's sake."* You can see right there that before Paul's sufferings ever began, Christ had **already** ordained this as part of Paul's repayment or punishment for all of those past wrongful actions against the Christians. We must remember though, that this is not all that God is. We must also realize that God's love is present also. You can see in the words of Ananias to Christ, that this Christian, who was obviously consecrating his life to Christ, needed confirmation that God was going to be perfectly just. It was important to the continuation and building of Ananias' faith to know that God wouldn't let Paul get away with murder. He needed that confirmation, and he got it.

126

Punishment For Sin Is Usually Delayed

The second point that we must remember when someone sins against us and hurts us, is that God's punishment often does not take place right away. It may initially look as though that person has gotten away with some horrible wrong toward us. We must remember that God's punishment is perfectly designed and perfectly timed, and it is consequently sometimes delayed to have its perfect effects in the life of an individual. When God does punish an individual, He does it in such a way as to fulfill His personal requirement for perfect judgment, for being the absolutely ethical judge of the universe. He also demonstrates his love for the individual that he punishes by providing punishment that will reveal the Lord to that person (Ezekiel 6:14, 7:9, 20:26, 24:24, 28:23, 28:26, 34:27). This will provide that individual with a maximal opportunity to turn his entire life around and to learn those life lessons necessary to become the kind of person that God wants him to be. This is a far different type of punishment than any of us could possibly inflict on anyone.

In Deuteronomy 32:35, Moses prophesies God's wrath upon the Jews because of their idolatrous practices: *"To me belongeth vengence, and recompense; their foot shall slide in due time: for the day of their calamity is at hand, and the things that shall come upon them make haste."* The phrase "in due time" is an important statement of the concept that God has a perfect time for every event, including punishment for sin.

We can see the delay between Paul's persecution of the Christians and his own punishment. When we study the Bible's description of the relationship between God and Paul, it seems as if God must have reasoned as follows. "Paul has done all those wrong things prior to his conversion. I've got to punish him, but I don't have to punish him immediately. If I have to punish him, I can wait until the times and situations in which many people will be converted through that

127

punishment. I will thus wait until that punishment can be turned into something good, both for Paul and the rest of Christendom.''

There was a long delay between King David's committing adultery with Bathsheba and arranging the death of her husband, and God's punishment of all that. David was punished through his own sinful acts being later repeated by his children against each other and against him. David had a son named Amnon who raped one of David's daughters named Tamar. Another of David's sons, Absolom, avenged this rape by killing Amnon. Later on, Absolom led a rebellion against Daivid. Absolom had intercourse with his father's concubines in order to demonstrate to the people that he was against his father. Absolom would have most likely killed David had he won that rebellion. We can thus see David's sins against others being committed or attempted against him much later in his life. Yet, the Lord ministered to him and saw him through it without David's life or effectiveness being destroyed. In 2 Samuel, Chapter 12, Nathan the prophet tells David of the future punishment that God will provide for his behavior with Uriah and Bathsheba. Here and in Psalm 51, we can see David's repentance and complete acceptance of whatever God wishes to provide. The outcome was that even though all these awful things happened to David, God permitted him to continue his reign. Even though David's sins were made public to all future generations, there has probably never been another king in history so admired as David. Whenever the Bible compares other kings to David, that king never measures up to him. David thus became the standard of excellence among kings. Only the incredible love and grace of God would have made that possible.

This concept that God's punishment is often delayed because of the perfection of God's plan is also revealed in Genesis, Chapter 15. We are basically told that God was going to punish the Amorite people, but that He wasn't going to do it until their iniquity (sinfulness) was full. Let me share portions of Genesis Chapter 15 with you.

> *"12 - And when the sun was going down, a deep sleep fell on Abram; and, lo, an horror of great darkness fell upon him.*
>
> *"13 - And he (God) said unto Abram, Know of a surety that thy seed shall be a stranger in a land that is not theirs, and shall serve them; and they shall afflict them four hundred years."*

Here God is giving Abram the prophecy of the future four hundred year enslavement of the Jews by the Egyptians.

> *"14 - And also that nation, whom they shall serve, will I judge: and afterward shall they come out with great substance.*
>
> *"15 - And thou shalt go to thy fathers in peace; thou shalt be buried in a good old age.*
>
> *"16 - But in the fourth generation they shall come hither again: for the iniquity of the Amorites is not yet full."*

God was telling Abraham right there that He was going to give his descendants this land that now belonged to the Amorites, but not until their sinfullness would increase to the point that they would have to be destroyed. At that future time, it would become a proper thing for this land to be taken away from the Amorites and put into the hands of Abraham's descendants without lending any questions to the perfection of God's judgments.

We can see there that God had some very important plans, but they were delayed, in this case for generations, because God knew what the Amorites were going to do in the future. It is important to remember that the Lord waits until the perfect time comes for His judgments to be executed in the lives of ourselves and others today, just as He has always done. We can see this same principle in the life of Jacob. Genesis, in Chapters 25 through 33, describes how the elder brother Esau sold his birthright to Jacob. Jacob wanted that birthright, for it would make him the primary descendant through which the family lineage would be recorded, as well as the spiritual leader and ruling head of his tribe. He approached Esau at a time when Esau was quite hungry, and offered him a bowl of soup in return for the birthright which was rightfully to go to Esau. Esau agreed to this. It was traditional that their father, Isaac, would confer the blessing upon the eldest son. Jacob and his mother, Rebecca, conspired to deceive aged, blind Isaac. They wrapped Jacob's arms with goatskin so that he would feel and smell like Esau. They succeeded in tricking Isaac into blessing Jacob under the pretense that he was Esau.

It appeared at that time that Jacob got away with the trick. But then he had to flee, because of the danger that Esau would subsequently kill him. Jacob went to Rebecca's brother, an uncle named Laban. Laban repetitively tricked Jacob for the next fourteen years. Laban initially tricked Jacob into marrying his relatively plain daughter, Leah, rather than the more beautiful Rachel. Laban repetitively tried to trick Jacob to receive smaller compensation for tending Laban's herds. Jacob, the trickster, thus became the recipient of trickery. Yet the Lord saw Jacob through all those experiences. When the time came for Jacob to return to his homeland, he left with both Leah and Rachel for his wives, with many children, and enough flocks to make him a wealthy man. This leads us to the next concept.

Tribulation Builds Character

The third point that we must remember when someone is sinning against us, is that God selects us as the object or recipient of sinful behavior from others, so as to build character in our lives. He punishes the other persons later. Whenever we experience a very distasteful situation in which someone has hurt us, it is thus important that we ask ourselves questions such as, "What is God trying to teach me?" "What test is He giving me to determine whether or not

I am ready for what He really wants to give me in terms of important jobs, experiences, relationships, or material provisions? What is God trying to build in me by this experience?'' Whenever we ask these questions in faith, we will always get the answers. Every time that I have asked these questions, either in my own life, or in the lives of those I have counselled, I have **always** received important answers.

When Jacob decided to return to his homeland, he sneaked away from Laban. On the way back to his homeland, the Bible tells us that Jacob met the angel of the Lord. Theologists speculate that this angel may have been Christ in a different body. It was necessary for Jacob to wrestle with the angel to obtain that blessing that he had sneaked from Isaac years before. Jacob received a lame thigh for the rest of his life during that fight.

Several important things happened in that transaction. The Bible says that they wrestled all night. It was a long wrestling match. This was probably a long, fearful ordeal for Jacob, who had persistently demonstrated cowardice in his life prior to this event. He was thus punished through this encounter and through the resulting disability, a lifelong limp. But he apparently walked away a different man. This was apparently the first time in his life that he really stood and fought for anything of great value. Jacob faced the danger that Esau might still be beligerent to him. Shortly after the wrestling match, Jacob met Esau face to face. Courage was built in Jacob through this wrestling match when he successfully wrestled this blessing from the angel of the Lord. The permanent limp that he received was nothing less than a badge of courage. Jacob's name was changed to Israel, which means, "He who wrestles with the Lord." In Genesis 32:28, the angel of the Lord told Jacob, *"Thy name shall be called no more Jacob, but Israel: for as a prince hast thou power with God and with men, and hast prevailed."* He was ready to face the danger that Esau might be beligerent to him in their meeting, which was shortly to occur. God used the punishment due Jacob as the means to build the character strength that would be needed by the leader of a great nation of people. Furthermore, that wrestling match produced a widespread admiration of Jacob for the rest of his life and to this day. We can thus see the love and wisdom of God in His punishment of Jacob.

We can see some of God's ways when we look at the history of the Jews in the Old Testament. King Nebuchadnezzar was directed by God to come against the Jews at certain times so as to refine them. Nebuchadnezzar refused to acknowledge that God was real or important when he captured the Jews. That did not prevent God from using him in God's refining of the Jews through their Babylonian enslavement. Later, at the proper time, God provided King Nebuchadnezzar seven years of psychosis, which was apparently necessary for the king to reject enough pride to become able to have a relationship with God.

I saw this refinement by tribulation occur in the life of a man who had a very successful career in corporate management. He was in middle age at the time that he sought consultation for a depression which had periodically recurred over the years. It had reached such severity that he felt that he now had to get something done about it. We reviewed his life, trying to determine what was causing this depression. This revealed that he had lost his father at an early age and had acquired a stepfather. The stepfather also had a son of his own. Throughout childhood, his stepfather had treated this stepson very differently from his own son, whom he had permitted to "get away with anything." Anything the real son wanted to do was fine. His father would not set limits for him. He would give him anything that he wanted to have. In contrast, the stepson often had to work for those things that he wanted. He had more difficult chores to do. Much more was expected of him. He grew to be a man who always bore resentment toward this stepfather. He felt that the stepfather had never really loved him as much as he loved that real son. This was always a real stumbling block for him. His bitterness about this had been causing enough depression to make him quite uncomfortable for many years. I asked him, "What happened to that man's real son?" He replied, "Well, he's a drunkard. He has never held a steady job for any significant period of time. Even now, though he has married and has children, he is still a financial parasite upon his father." That boy's father now felt forced to continue treating him the same way that he had erroneously treated him throughout his childhood. On the other hand, this stepson, who was depressed about all that, had become an important member of his community, had good relationships with the Lord and with his family. He had a very successful occupational history, and was generally doing quite well. When he was confronted with these facts regarding what had been built in his life through all of that childhood "unfairness," he suddenly rejected the bitterness. His depression was then healed! He had simply never realized that one of the best things that the Lord had ever done for him was to keep him **out** of the position of that stepfather's real son, who was spoiled and ruined by lack of discipline. The very thing about which he had been bitter had been used by God to build strong character and ability into his life!

In Hebrews, Chapter 12, the Bible teaches in the following verses that it is important the the Lord chasten us. *"5 - And ye have forgotten the exhortation which speaketh unto you as unto children, My son, despise not thou the chastening of the Lord, nor faint when thou art rebuked of him: 6 - For whom the Lord loveth he chasteneth, and scourgeth every son whom he receiveth. 7 - If ye endure chastening, God dealeth with you as with sons: for what son is he whom the father chasteneth not?"* Verse 11 continues, *"Now no chastening for the present seemeth to be joyous, but grievous: nevertheless afterward it yieldeth the peaceable fruit of righteousness unto them which are exercised thereby."*

As a psychiatrist, I seldom have the opportunity to make first hand observations of parents disciplining their children. I must usually obtain this information by interviewing several members of troubled families. On one occasion, however, my wife and I visited in the home of someone we knew, who lived in a small town. This woman had several preschool children who had acquired a reputation in that town of being extremely undisciplined. In conversation, the woman mentioned that her own mother could babysit the children only rarely, "because she couldn't take them for more than an hour once in a while." Observing the interaction between the woman and her children during the visit proved very interesting. Throughout the visit in their living room, the children continually ran and jumped on the couch and on chairs, at times removing pillows off the couch and throwing them on the floor as well as at us. Small decorative objects and accent pieces throughout the well furnished living room were constantly removed by the children. A set of encyclopedias was likewise removed from the bookcase and strewn about the floor. Their mother picked up behind them throughout our visit. Of every dozen inappropriate actions of the children, the mother corrected them approximately twice. The rest of the time, she would look at what they were doing and smile at them! She was thus subconsciously communicating to the children that she **approved** of their misbehaving. Her failure to discipline her children one hundred percent of the time was thus actively ruining their characters. God is a better parent than that! No one likes to be punished for sin. Yet, we must realize that without God's punishment of our sins, the knowledge that He would let us get away with anything we wanted to do would ruin us. We would most likely all become hopeless reprobates.

God's purpose in permitting us to endure hardship is also illustrated in his relationship with the Jews, whom he permitted to be sinned against by many nations. Zechariah 13:8-9 teaches, *"And it shall come to pass, that in all the land, saith the Lord, two parts therein shall be cut off and die; but the third shall be left therein. 9 - And I will bring the third part through the fire, and will refine them as silver is refined, and will try them as gold is tried: they shall call on my name, and I will hear them: I will say, It is my people: and they shall say, The Lord is my God."* Undisciplined children grow to resent their parents. Their parents come to feel contempt for their incorrigible children. God does not want that kind of contemptible relationship with **His** children, nor do we want that kind of relationship with Him.

Conclusion

In conclusion, whenever someone sins against us, we must remember these concepts.

First: No sin goes unpunished. God isn't going to permit himself to be made a liar by the rotten sins of somebody who is trying to hurt us. He has promised us that He is going to punish every sin, and He has got to do that to maintain His perfect system of ethics. God must maintain His perfect judgship of the Universe, and yet carry out His promise to love each person enough to provide that discipline which the Father must provide.

Second: We must remember that God's punishment is perfectly timed and designed. We should not be fooled by the fact that God's punishment of someone who sins against us is often not immediate. It doesn't have to be immediate — God is not worried about immediacy. He is only worried about perfection: perfection of His system of justice, perfection of everything that He does, and perfect fulfillment of each of His promises. Anyone who thus sees what God has done would feel a need to worship the Lord rather than scorn Him. We must remember that God's punishment is often delayed, because God wants to use that punishment to reveal Himself to the sinner in such a way as to give that person a maximum opportunity to get right with God, right with his fellow man, and right with himself.

Third: Whenever God permits another person to sin against us, we must remember to ask, "What is God trying to build in me by letting this happen to me at this moment? In what ways is He trying to increase my strength of mind, body and spirit? If that person had to sin against somebody, why did God let me be in his path at this moment?'' We must also ask, "How might God be testing me to see whether my character, emotional strength, and wisdom have developed adequately for me to be able to receive even greater things that He wants to give to me?'' Each time that God completes a state of refinement in a Christian's life, that person becomes better able to receive and demonstrate the fruits of a personal relationship with Christ: peace, joy, and a productive life!

8

Successful Christian Relationships Between Men and Women In Life Today

Few subjects are more difficult for Christians or others to understand than are the Bible's instructions for proper relationships between husbands and wives. There is a great deal of controversy regarding the place of women in Christian life. It is taught from some pulpits that women should not preach in the church. Other preachers emphasize the important roles which women played in worship and spiritual leadership during Biblical times. Paul's writings give the conditions under which women ought to prophesy in church, such as that they should have their heads covered (1 Corinthians 11:5). In Joel 2:28-29, the Bible teaches *"And it shall come to pass afterward, that I will pour out my spirit upon all flesh; and your sons and your daughters shall prophesy, your old men shall dream dreams, your young men shall see visions: 29 - And upon the servants and upon the handmaids in those days will I pour out my spirit."* The Bible makes it clear that God does not withhold the gifts of His Holy Spirit from females.

A partial list of the many examples in the Scriptures of prophetesses would include Rachel, Miriam, Deborah (who was not only a prophetess, but also one of the Judges of Israel) Huldah, Noadiah, Isaiah's wife, Elizabeth, Mary the mother of Jesus, Anna, and Phillip's four daughters. Though Pilate's wife is not called a prophetess in the Bible, she came to Pilate as he was about to render his judgment of Christ, and told him that she had a dream which informed her that it was wrongful for Christ to be crucified (Matthew 27:19).

Difference Does Not Imply Inferiority

It is clear, however, that the Bible treats men and women differently. The fact that different instructions are given for the two sexes is very disturbing for many **modern** people who want to treat the two sexes identically. Nowhere does the Bible downgrade women. It just indicates that men and women are different, and that they need different instructions by which to live.

In the practice of psychiatry, when I am speaking to a woman, I am speaking to a totally different type of personality than when I am speaking to a man. The two sexes are simply not the same. They think, feel, and respond differently to identical situations. They have different sets of hormones at work in their bodies, and they have different attitudes about given subjects. I have had the privilege of observing many relationships between men and women who followed Biblical instructions for those relationships, in contrast to many who departed from those instructions.

The Protective Quality of God's Instructions

A middle aged housewife came for consultation in a crisis situation in which she felt emotionally at the end of her rope. Her brother had recently committed suicide. She said that she felt a great deal of despair, because he had called her shortly before he committed suicide and asked her to bring him to the state asylum. He had indicated that he was somewhere in the local skid row area at the time. He had demonstrated a number of severe emotional problems, including a lack of conscience. His psychopathic lifestyle had created many problems for this woman, as well as for his entire extended family. She had consequently refused to bring him to the

138

asylum. She had told him, "My husband has instructed me that I am to have no further contact with you, because of the amount of harm that has come to me in the past whenever I associated with you." The next thing that she told me was that he had committed suicide, and she felt terrible about it. She then indicated that her husband loved her brother, but that he had been forced to reach that conclusion because the brother had caused her to experience severe emotional problems on several previous occasions. It had thus proven to be disastrous for her to have contact with her brother.

Without any further information, I showed her Ephesians 5:22-23, *"Wives, submit yourselves unto your own husbands, as unto the Lord. 23 - For the husband is the head of the wife, even as Christ is the head of the church: and he is the saviour of the body."* I told her that she had done what her husband had said to do, and she had consequently done what God had said to do; so I knew that what she had done was somehow right, because of my previous experiences with the results of following God's instructions in my life and in the lives of my patients. I pointed out to her that if her brother had really wanted to get to the state asylum, he could have gotten there without her, even if he had hitchhiked. In view of the history of her having had such bad experiences in her relationships with him, it was quite likely that he had been trying to involve her in his problems for unhealthy reasons.

She then replied, "I am sure he could have gotten to the asylum. As a matter of fact, before he killed himself, he went to Europe and shot himself there. Several thousand dollars were found on his person after his death." She added that on another past occasion, she had in fact brought him to the asylum during one of his emotional crises. It was necessary for him to be committed to the hospital against his will. At that time, he promised her that he would kill her when he got out. We now faced the fact that within a short time after her brother had recently called her, a gun was found on his body.

We don't know what would have happened had she brought her brother to the asylum. We do know that he had adequate means to hire a cab to bring him there, so he really didn't need her for that purpose. The fact that he went to Europe rather than going to the hospital suggests that he wasn't terribly enthusiastic about going to the asylum.

It may very well be that this woman's life was spared by following her husband's instructions to have no further contact with her brother. The protective quality of these scriptural instructions for wives in relating to their husbands repetitively comes to my attention in my work as I see what happens in these relationships when those instructions are followed, as well as when they are rejected.

Consequences of Liberation

We are living in a day in which many people want personal freedom. Many want to be liberated. Many want to "do their own thing," so to speak. It is my observation, both in looking at life in my consulting room and in looking at history, that the "liberated" personality who feels free to do whatever he wishes is inevitably headed for a personal disaster, whether that person is male or female. The "liberated" personality is in rebellion against all authority, and is operating under compulsion rather than with sound judgment, versatility, and wisdom. The "liberated" personality is in bondage to this rebellion against authority. Such a "liberated" personality is likely to do whatever he or she "feels like doing," rather than following the instructions of God, parents, or the law. Such an individual is likely to experience chronic bitterness because of childhood rejection from parents. That individual is quite likely to be subconsciously transferring his bitterness towards parents to everyone else. If the childhood bitterness was felt toward the parent of the opposite sex, the bitterness may be mainly transferred to adults of the opposite sex in the present. If the childhood bitterness was felt toward a parent of the same sex, the adult may demonstrate a tremendous amount of bitter feelings and behavior toward people of the same sex in adult life.

Because of childhood rejection, children often feel a great deal of mistrust of parents. In adult life, they are then likely to mistrust all authority. This negative, bitter, mistrustful attitude towards parents gets transferred directly to one's perception of God and self. An individual in this position rejects the counsel or wisdom of other people. He often repeats his own errors as a result of a refusal to learn, even from his own experiences, when the obvious lessons of his tragedies are in conflict with what he wants to do.

Liberated Men

It is very interesting to look at what has happened to liberated, famous men in history who ran their lives on self will, without concern for God's will. Alexander the Great conquered much of the known world of his time. He died at the young age of thirty-three; yet, by the time of his death, he had already demonstrated severe bouts of alcoholism as well as an inclination for homosexual relationships. He murdered his best friend during a drunken rage. Even though he died so early in his adult life, he had already begun traveling a road that was filled with tragedy.

Julius Caesar was emperor of the Roman Empire. He had himself declared a god. He was scorned by contemporaries, because of being effeminate and homosexual. His life was ended by assassination. His closest friend, Brutus, was among his assassins.

Napoleon Bonaparte became emperor of the French Empire. Each of his two separate reigns terminated in horrible military disaster. He demonstrated an absolute compulsion to conquer and to become ruler of the world. By the time he ended his second reign, and his last series of military campaigns, he had destroyed the youth of France. Because the young adult population of Frenchmen had been decimated during his campaigns, he had resorted to waging his wars with the teenage male population of France. He spent the last years of life despairing in exile, where he made an unsuccessful suicide attempt by poisoning himself.

Adolph Hitler was another example of a man who did anything that he wanted to do. He scorned Christ for being a Jew. His attempt to become a world dictator by his vicious lack of either restraint or decency finally destroyed his own nation. He ended his life by suicide after winning the contempt even of future generations.

The Secret Power of Feminine Influence

It seems apparent that the liberated personality is not one that produces good things for one's personal life. When women read the Scriptural instructions for relationships between women and men, they often fail to understand the power that is present in a woman's submissive attitude toward a man. These scriptural instructions are based on God's knowledge of how men think. The first love in a man's life is his mother. Down deep in a man's heart is a yearning to have a woman really love him, care about his needs, and respect him as a person of value, the way his mother did in childhood. A man will do anything to get these things. A woman who approaches a man with a non-threatening attitude, communicating that she is truly interested in his welfare, can get anything that she wants from that man. Very few women understand this secret. Women who don't understand this often try to get what they want by progressively aggressive, offensive attitudes toward their husbands. Even though a man may have great social status, economic, political, or financial power, he is relatively reluctant to reject a woman whom he loves. Whenever the woman he loves treats him with disrespect, he tends to either retreat from the relationship or to form a mental wall between them. Men usually respond to disrespect or verbal assault from their wives by progressive non-involvement in their relationships with them.

The main complaints of women today about their marriages seems to be, "My husband is not enthusiastic about me anymore. He is not enthusiastic about spending time with me. He is not enthusiastic about talking to me. He is not even enthusiastic about sex anymore. He is not enthusiastic about participating in the decisions regarding the family's life, not even in finances, what we're going to buy, or what we're going to do about vacations or entertainment. He's just there, and that's about all.''

The history of such relationships usually reveals that the man may have had a tendency to select a wife who is hostile or disrespectful toward males. Something may have gone wrong in the relationship sometime in the past, and the woman began to get progressively aggressive verbally. She became progressively disrespectful and bitter, even to the point of getting verbally destructive. She may have become downgrading and critical of her husband to the point that he felt progressively like a nothing. He felt like he was getting cut down, so he just began operating like a non-functioning, psychologically castrated male. He then began playing the role of a functionally destroyed man in his marriage and family life.

The historical importance of women regarding their influence upon their husbands is clearly revealed throughout the Bible. It is interesting that Satan originally attacked Adam through Eve. He could have proceeded in any way that he wished. We must assume that he probably did it in a way that he knew would be most likely to be effective. Rather than making a direct, frontal, spiritual assault upon Adam, Satan defeated him through his wife.

Samson demonstrated incredible physical strength, and was a judge of Israel. In spite of his great power, he permitted Delilah to destroy him. The account of Samson and Delilah in Judges, Chapter 16, reveals that Delilah made multiple obvious attempts to destroy him by delivering him to the Philistines, before she finally succeeded. Rather than rejecting this woman who had such evil intentions toward him, mighty Samson permitted his relationship with Delilah to continue until he was essentially destroyed by it.

The Book of Esther is a tremendous example of the great influence of women over their husbands. Esther was selected by King Ahazuerus as one of his many wives, but she was his favorite wife and his queen. King Ahazuerus had been misled by Haman, who was the equivalent of a prime minister. Haman had succeeded in obtaining the King's approval of a plan to destroy all of the Jews in the Kingdom. Haman did not know that Esther was Jewish. Esther approached the King with a submissive attitude, and told him that Haman's plot would destroy her too, since she was Jewish. The king responded by preserving the Jews and ordering the hanging of Haman. The powerful King Ahazuerus had a reputation for being vicious. He was once approached by a man who wanted to keep his son out of military duty. The man offered him a sum of money to keep his son out of the army. The King ordered his guards to cut the man's son in half and then paraded his army between the two halves of the man's son. This is the kind of man with whom Esther was dealing. Yet, by demonstrating an adherence to the Bible's instructions for a wife's conduct toward her husband, she was able to get this king to do what she wanted, preventing the destruction of the Jews.

The Bible says that God made King Solomon the wisest king who would ever live, second only to the Messiah Himself! Solomon obtained a total of 700 wives and 300 concubines, violating God's instructions in Deuteronomy 17:17 regarding the kings of Israel, *"Neither shall he multiply wives to himself, that his heart not turn away (from God)."* Toward the latter portion of Solomon's life, he permitted his heathen wives to influence him to worship their false gods. He even built altars to their heathen gods. One of the world's wisest kings thus entered the practice of idolatry, in response to the influence of his wives! This is another example of the tremendous power that women have in their relationships with their husbands. That reality is a direct contrast to the way that the average woman perceives her relationship with her husband.

When Pontius Pilate's wife told him that she had realized through a dream that it would be a very wrong thing for him to crucify Christ, Pilate initially accepted her counsel (Matthew Chapter 27). He began to try to spare Christ, but he became fearful of the crowds who demanded that Jesus be crucified. He could have told the crowds, "No. I won't give you this man. You can't have him, because he's innocent." Instead, he told them to do as they wished, because of fear of what the crowd might do. He apparently feared the Jews would complain to the Roman Emperor about his conduct if he obstructed the crucifixion of a man reputed to be a king of the Jews. Pilate thus went on historical records as being the man to crucify Christ. Even though the Bible makes it clear that he didn't want to do it, the average person thinks of Pilate as the man who was responsibile for the crucifixion of Christ.

Obstacles To Successful Relationships
Between The Sexes

Certain things commonly go wrong in relationships between men and women. The Bible has given us instructions which, when followed, will produce peace, joy, and fruitfulness in the relationships between husbands and wives. Yet, an incredible amount of discord and despair often takes place in marriages. Certain common psychological obstacles, or snares, rob relationships of joy.

Negative Parental Transference

The first snare, or trap, that often destroys relationships between the sexes is called **negative parental transference**. The individual who experiences this problem had a bad childhood relationship with the parent of the opposite sex. He consequently grew up feeling that anybody of that sex is eventually going to somehow do him in. All of that person's childhood bitterness toward that parent gets transferred to his or her spouse in adult life. While this occurs to both sexes, it happens much more commonly to women than to men. The probable reason is that it is more common for fathers to reject their children than for mothers to do so. In psychiatric practice, I certainly see many cases of mothers having rejected their children. Yet, it is statistically more traditional for women to be relatively involved in the care of their children, whereas it is almost a tradition for a large minority of men to be much less involved with their children than are the mothers. Some men are almost totally unable to relate to their children. This goes back to these fathers having been rejected in their own childhoods. Such men can often relate to their children after the children become late adolescents or adults, but they simply cannot relate to children. Following the examples of their own fathers, they feel as if it is not manly to demonstrate affection or to play with children. Their daughters often become adults who resent their husbands because these women expect all men to reject them.

Rebellious Spirit

The second snare that destroys the goodness of a relationship between a husband and a wife is a rebellious spirit. A rebellious spirit is usually the result of mistrust. One important subconscious fear and question in the minds of people with this problem is, "What's going to happen if I trust somebody important to me?" Such a person feels that his parents let him down or rejected him in childhood, so it is expected that everyone will let him down. Chronic bitterness about such childhood experiences may produce a rebellious personality. This bitterness produces a hostile tendency to rebel and to do the opposite of what people expect of one. Such a rebellious personality problem is one of the most deadly poisons to relationships that I have seen.

Members of either sex may demonstrate rebellious personalities. In my experience, psychological rebellion

146

through verbal interaction is more commonly demonstrated by women, whereas behavioral rebellion is more common with men. Women with this problem may verbally object to and oppose everything their husbands do or say. Such women often play the roles of "castrating females." When men want to demonstrate a rebellious spirit, it is often done through either alcoholism or gambling. Both sexes may demonstrate such rebellion by means of unfaithfulness or adultery.

Adultery

The third snare that destroys relationships between husbands and wives is adultery. We are living in a day where this is a very popular form of behavior. Many people are living by philosophies such as the following. "There's no real right and wrong. The Bible is outmoded." Few things are more devastating to a marriage than one of the marital partners discovering that the other has engaged in adultery. I have seen many people who developed severe emotional illnesses and many who became psychotic when they discovered the adultery of their spouses. The destructiveness of this phenomenon to both partners in the marriage is quite impressive. I have also seen many people who became psychotic or severely depressed in response to their own adultery. Even more impressive is the tremendous, unexpected psychological devastation that occurs to the children in these families when adultery occurs. I have seen many adults whose lives have been psychologically ruined because of their reactions to having witnessed adulterous behavior on the part of one of their parents during childhood. In many of these cases, they didn't witness the sexual activity, but witnessed the associated flirtation or secret meetings with the knowledge that their parent was going to or already did commit adultery. Life long depression, anxiety, guilt, and hatred of self and others often occurs in the children who witness or learn about such behavior on the part of their parents.

Alcoholism

The fourth snare that destroys the goodness of marriage relationships is alcoholism. Frequent discussions occur regarding the question of whether alcoholism is a disease or a sin. The psychiatric evaluations that I have performed in cases of alcoholism usually reveal that alcoholic behavior is a means of expressing chronic bitterness. The alcoholic is usually bitter about childhood rejection or abuse that he or she received from parents. An adult with this childhood background may also be receiving chronic verbal or psychological abuse from a spouse. The drunkenness often provides an excuse for hostile behavior and reduces the likelihood that others will retaliate when the drunkard sobers up and apologizes. A person who destroys his or her family's welfare by means of drunkenness is likely to be tolerated for a much longer period of time than is someone sober who engages in inappropriate verbal, physical, or financial transactions.

There also appears to be some hereditary tendency for many to be unable to handle alcohol. There is no hereditary tendency to choose to take the first drink of alcohol, but rather a hereditary tendency to be unable to control oneself once one begins using it. The alcoholic can decide, if he chooses, "I am not going to drink anymore, because alcohol destroys other things which are far more important to me." What usually causes the trouble is the simple refusal to avoid even the first drink, because of the amount of the bitterness that alcoholics feel toward people. The alcoholic individual usually has a helpless-child self image, in spite of the fact that he may in reality be an immensely successful person who holds important positions socially, vocationally, financially, or politically. Yet, down deep, he may feel like a nothing, or a helpless child who is unable to handle himself in stressful situations.

The individual who is demonstrating alcoholism usually has a very poor relationship with God. He feels and acts as

148

though he cannot trust God, and cannot really turn his life over to God. He feels that he must face stress by relying upon the alcohol rather than upon God. Alcoholism is thus a spiritual illness.

Psychotic Behavior

The fifth snare to good relationships between husbands and wives is that of psychosis. The joy of many marriages is obliterated through one of the marital partners repetitively demonstrating psychotic breaks. As in the problem of alcoholism, the moral and philosophical question arises, "To what extent is this a sickness, and to what extent is it plain, old, sinful behavior?" Psychotic individuals are usually engaged in incredibly destructive behavior. Such individuals often have to be physically restrained and locked up in order to prevent their destroying somebody else or themselves.

The form of a psychosis in progress is strikingly similar to an adult temper tantrum. Everyone has at times observed a distressed mother dragging a screaming three or four year old child out of a store's toy department because the child didn't get the toy that he or she wanted. Everybody in the store is looking at her to see why the mother is abusing her screaming child. The psychotic adult often behaves like such a child who is kicking and dragging his feet.

My psychiatric evaluations of people who have a history of psychotic breaks have revealed a typical pattern. These people usually harbor a high level of conscious or subconscious bitterness toward parents who rejected or abused them during childhood. Such people demonstrate a tremendous amount of unforgiveness. The combination of chronic bitterness towards parents in the absence of forgiveness to resolve that bitterness is a very explosive mixture.

Compulsive Gambling

The sixth snare that destroys the kind of relationship

between men and women that God wants to give them, is the phenomenon of compulsive gambling. Compulsive gambling appears to be more commonly a male phonomenon, though it is sometimes demonstrated by women. Compulsive gamblers periodically destroy their family finances, often placing the family deeply in debt. They may not only gamble away everything they have, but also as much as they can borrow. Like the alcoholic and the psychotic, the compulsive gambler is often replaying feelings of chronic bitterness towards parents who rejected him during childhood. Rather than forgiving his parents, he transfers his bitterness to his spouse and even to his children. He subconsciously hopes to resolve the resulting guilt by financially ruining himself in the process of expressing so much bitterness toward others. The compulsive gambler often suffers from chronic guilt regarding past sins for which he feels unforgiven. Recognizing that guilt, confessing the sins, accepting Christ's forgiveness, and forgiving rejecting parents heals the compulsive gambling.

These are some of the common obstacles that cause people to reject the kind of relationships that God wanted men and women to share when He provided His instructions for the relationships between husbands and wives in the Bible.

Conclusion

In conclusion, it is important to realize that even many of the most powerful men in history have been totally shipwrecked when they tried to lead "liberated" lives. Their conduct of their lives by only their self will, without concern for what God wanted them to do, obviously did not provide them peace. In the Book of Ecclesiastes, Solomon enumerates the various pleasures that a person can have in life. He emphasizes that one ought to enjoy his life. But after he discusses the various pleasures that an individual can have in life, he concludes with statements such as the following verses in Ecclesiastes, Chapter 12.

"8 - Vanity of vanities, saith the preacher; all is vanity."
"11 - The words of the wise are as goads, and as nails fastened by the masters of assemblies, which are given from one shepherd. 12 - And further, by these, my son, be admonished: of making many books there is no end; and much study is a weariness of the flesh. 13 - Let us hear the conclusion of the whole matter: Fear God, and keep his commandments: for this is the whole duty of man. 14 - For God shall bring every work into judgment, with every secret thing, whether it be good, or whether it be evil." Here King Solomon, a man with more wealth, power, and wisdom than anyone could want, concludes that after considering all that life can offer, knowing God's commandments and following them are the only things of real and lasting value.

It has been my experience in observing large numbers of lives, that knowing and following the scriptural instructions for successful relationships between men and women produces peace, joy, and fruitfulness in marriage. When these instructions are rejected, we end up with what we see in our society today, with the divorce rate continually escalating, and with family life as we have known it being decimated.

Many women respond with anger to the Biblical instructions for the conduct of women toward their husbands. They think, "What are you, a male chauvinist? You mean I ought to be careful of what I say to my husband?" When many women dislike something that their husbands say or do, they impulsively say, "Let me tell it like it is," and proceed to bitterly criticize their husbands. They overlook the power of a submissive, respectful, caring attitude toward husbands. The bottom line of the issue is, "What works to produce success?" Women want influence in getting what they want and need from their husbands. They also want the respect and love of their husbands. They should never overlook the fact that deep down, their husbands feel and experience the marital relationship as little boys who want mother's love more than anything else in the

151

world. Men will do almost anything to obtain that kind of love and care. A man's natural tendency is therefore to say "Yes" to his wife's requests. Likewise, a man's tendency is to say "No" to someone who treats him with disrespect or contempt.

9

Successful Christian Parenting

Being a psychiatrist seems rather easy compared to the occasionally complex demands of being a parent. It is very striking that people may become trained to be psychiatrists, but people usually don't receive training to be parents. Much is at stake when one's own children are involved. If one knows what can go wrong with children and how it may affect them in later life, parenting can be more demanding at times.

Parents feel many common worries. "What's going to happen to my children? How are they going to turn out? Look at what's happening to so many other children who reach their teens, or who reach early adult life and experience so much tragedy. How can I keep my children out of the drug scene, or the homosexual scene? Or the destructive sexual promiscuity and adultery that many people practice? Or the high divorce rate?" The moral and behavioral standards of society have been progressively disintegrating for the past several generations. It is a very difficult time to be a parent, because we no longer have the help of society in leading our children in the right directions. In fact, the opposite condition prevails. This places a much greater burden of responsibility on parents. Parents must have an impact on children that will help them to be different from everyone around them in those ways that will help them, and that will prevent them from sharing the tragic lifestyles of so many people in today's society.

It is unfortunate that so many young people in their late teens and early twenties reject the counsel and wisdom of their parents. Parents often see the erroneous decisions and choices that their children are making and want to protect them from the consequences that they are about to suffer. For example, some parents discover that an eighteen year old child has entered the homosexual community, and they become fearful of what is going to happen to that child. He may go to a psychiatrist's office simply to satisfy the parents. He may even ask the psychiatrist to telephone his parents and say, "Don't worry about it, just because this child is homosexual. He (or she) is going to be alright." Young people often think, "After all, so many people are living this way nowadays and are taking a stand for it, it must not be all bad." A similar situation exists regarding the drug scene. Many young people are on drugs, though their parents object. They think, "So many people are on drugs, it must be alright. **All** my friends use drugs." Many young people are having similar experiences in marriage today. They may suddenly decide that they simply don't want to be married anymore, in spite of the fact that they already have children involved in the marriage. Their own parents often realize that these young adults are about to experience a series of awful tragedies, and the parents want to protect them. But the young adults often decide, "I don't think that my parents are right. Everybody else is getting a divorce. It must not be **that** bad. Why not do it too? If it feels good, do it." Incredible numbers of people are entering into serious trouble living nowadays by making choices which they believe will be alright because so many other people are doing these things. They don't realize that the other people who are doing these things are experiencing many unfortunate consequences of which they do not tell. People like to tell the world about it when they feel they are winners. But should they suddenly realize they have become terrible losers, they are much more likely to become silent. Because young people do not realize this, they often must learn from bitter and painful experiences of their own, rather than learning from the experiences of others.

One of the real difficulties about parenting is that children seem silently accepting of things going wrong in the early years, from birth to eleven years of age. Then they enter the adolescent years, from twelve to eighteen years of age. In that stage, everything that went wrong from birth to adolescence suddenly explodes in the faces of children, and it explodes in the faces of parents, teachers, or anyone involved in the lives of the children. Pre-adolescent children can be beaten, verbally abused and rejected, and are likely to accept it quietly. Until approximately eleven years of age, children will accept such treatment while manifesting few symptoms besides mediocre scholastic work or excessive fighting with peers. When they enter adolescence, their identities begin changing. They are no longer children. They are no longer adults. At the adolescent stage, the identity is thus normally in a very uncertain state. If the adolescent has suffered parental rejection or verbal abuse during earlier years, all of the anger and bitterness that has been building up in his mind may be suddenly released and expressed in his verbal and physical behavior. The result is often so explosive that the adolescent may have to be committed to an asylum in order to recover his emotional health. Prior to this, the parents may have thought that everything was fine!

I would like to present several guiding principles regarding the relationships between parents and children. These principles can be used to effectively guide one's parenting in a general but important way. One could write for months and years on fine points of parenting, regarding what to do in small situations; but what parents need most are **general** guidelines or directions. If one makes a small mistake and mishandles a small matter, children are usually very forgiving of parents. Errors and even blunders can be straightened out, as long as there is no global or repetitive misdirection in the relationship between the parent and the child.

The three most important principles of effective parenting that I can communicate are as follows: communication to the child of affection or acceptance, realization that the child is identifying with his parents' character and behavior, and teaching the child respect for authority. This last point may seem very old fashioned in today's world. I find myself amused at the fact that though people have been successfully rearing children for so many centuries, some authorities on child behavior will periodically assert that parents should do exactly the opposite of what effective parents have always done. Today's children are mostly like children of previous generations, in spite of the fact that they are sometimes subjected to trying and dangerous situations.

Communication Of Affection And Acceptance To The Child

Violation of the first principle of successful parenting, the communication of affection and acceptance, is probably one of the most common causes of emotional disturbances of childhood and adolescence. It is very important to children that they feel that both parents love them and accept them. The reason this is so important is that children derive their self images from what they perceive that their parents feel about them. Children are in a state of perpetual hypnosis regarding their parents, in the sense that they tend to feel that their parents are always right. This is a basic characteristic of childhood, particularly prior to adolescence. If a child is perceiving rejection from a parent, the child is likely to assume that the parent is right to reject him. The outcome of this is that the child begins feeling like a basically unlovable, bad person. The inevitable conclusion is, "If my own mother or father can't love me, who can?" Rejected children usually experience a great deal of chronic bitterness. They feel bitter, not only because they have been rejected by their parents, but also because they feel that there is no hope for them to be valued, loved, or respected. This lack of hope produces despair.

The child who feels unloved by parents is likely to feel no love for himself: that is, he is likely to have no self respect. In Matthew 22:35-40, a Pharisee asked Christ which is the great commandment in the law (Good News Bible). *"37 - Jesus answered, 'Love the Lord your God with all your heart, with all your soul, and with all your mind. 38 - This is the greatest and the most important commandment. 39 - The second most important commandment is like it: Love your neighbor as yourself. 40 - The whole law of Moses and the teachings of the prophets depend on these two commandments.' "* Christ included the commandment to love yourself. A person must love himself, not in a vain or self-centered way; but he must respect himself as a creation of God and as a child of God. A person who lacks self respect is unable to relate to anyone successfully. The only way that any of us can relate to anyone else is from the self. We must first perceive ourselves in attempting to relate to someone else. If we perceive ourselves as basically worthless, then it is very hard for us to expect that anyone else will think very much of us. Lack of self respect causes an expectation of being rejected. When people expect to be rejected by everyone, they tend to begin retaliating even before the rejection takes place. The end result is a ruined or absent social life and an inability to participate in adult family life.

Many men have the erroneous attitude that it is not masculine to express affection, even to their children. They fail to realize how important they are to their children. This usually results from their own fathers having been inhibited in expressing affection. This unfortunate attitude should be replaced with a new awareness of the importance of their roles and attitudes toward their children.

Another common cause of parental failure to express love and affection to children is that the parents never received affection from either of their own parents. Because they were rejected by their own parents, they expect to be rejected by everyone. Rather than risk expressing affection and receiving rejection again, they avoid the problem by avoiding any admission of affection to anyone.

In my experience, when parents come to understand the importance to their children of their expressing affection to them, even if the parents have somewhat of a struggle with this, they can work toward a gradually increasing expression of affection. Many parents don't realize how important it is to their children that they verbally and behaviorally express love for them, and the problem is never addressed. Children equate parents spending time with them with parents loving them. In the child's mind, "If my mother never spends time with me, my mother doesn't love me. If my father never spends time with me, my father doesn't love me." This is a universal way that children think. They are usually quite correct. Mothers and fathers can usually spend as much time with their children as they wish. They are free, in the child's mind, to do anything they want to do. These great big parents can do things the child can't do, and they seem to have enormous power, knowledge, and abilities! They could certainly spend time with the child if they felt it were important. If parents understand how children are perceiving and interpreting what is being done in the parent-child relationship, it is usually easy to know what to do in most situations.

Identification

The second important principle of successful parenting involves awareness of and response to the problem of identification. What you **are** is what you are going to get from your children. As they observe parental personality, character, and behavior in their presence, they reproduce these qualities in their own personalities, characters, and actions. This phenomenon of children identifying with parents is one of the most powerful things that I have seen in personality development. I seldom see an emotional problem in the practice of psychiatry in which the phenomenon of identification is not a very important cause of that problem. People experience very powerful convictions that they must be like their parents in order to be okay, successful people. This is a very awesome thing! When I realize that my children are going to be what they see me being, it has a very deep effect on my behavior. There have been times when I have been tempted to do things that I refused to do, because I knew that my children would identify with what they see me portraying. The awareness of the effect of our behavior on our children is thus an important aid to parenting. We can apply this awareness to our choices of emotional, verbal, and behavioral responses to the situations that we face daily.

Many parents demonstrate a tendency to emotionally "fall apart" whenever stress comes. Such a parent's children see that and identify with it. It is extremely common for adults to obtain consultation for chronic anxiety or depression which is caused by feeling that they can't handle stress. This is a very great impairment. Many adults feel like helpless children in the face of stress. Many children observe a parent demonstrate fear or severe anxiety every time that stressful situations occur. Such a child is likely to become an adult who at some level of his mind, feels that he cannot handle stress. That child is likely to experience chronic anxiety and depression, because it is very depressing to feel that way in response to stress.

The problem of alcoholism effectively demonstrates the importance of identification in childhood development. One of the most common problems in treating alcoholism is that alcoholics often refuse to believe that they are alcoholics. Such people have usually had one or two alcoholic parents. I have interviewed many heavy drinkers who drank as much as their parents. While readily admitting that their parents were alcoholics, many of them steadfastly deny being alcoholics themselves. When confronted with this discrepancy, the conversation goes something like the following: "You're telling me that your father was alcoholic. You drink as much as he did, you get drunk as often as you do, and yet you're telling me that you are not an alcoholic. How can you be telling me that?'' The response is something like, "Well, you know, my father had to miss work a lot. I don't miss any work. I only get drunk on the nights when I don't have to work the next morning." Or, "I only get drunk when I'm at home. My father was unable to stay out of bars. That proves I'm not addicted to alcohol the way he was. I can control myself.''

It is amazing to see how the mind plays tricks on people, to tell them that they really are different from a parent, when in reality, they are doing the same things their parents did. This applies not only to alcoholism, but to everything. If children see their parents constantly fighting, they are likely to become adults who continually provoke fights with their spouses. People say that if you want to know how people are going to relate to a spouse, then find out what each person's relationship was like with the parent of the opposite sex. You can assume that their subsequent relationship with a spouse will probably be the same. It is thus very important that we realize that our children are going to be what they see us to be, rather than what we merely tell them to be.

Respect For Authority

The third very important principle in effective parenting is to teach children respect for authority. This is extremely important, because every one of us has a subconscious mind. It is very frightening to consider that each of us has a mind that will run our lives and even wreck our lives, without our having any awareness whatsoever of what that mind is thinking or feeling. This is an awesome fact; yet, it is a condition of human life that each of us must face. If we simply do whatever we feel like doing, we are likely to ruin our lives by giving the subconscious mind dominion over us. The people who avoid unfortunate decisions, choices, and

160

behavior are those who can short-circuit that subconscious mind and nullify its effect as a determinant of how we live. How can we short-circuit the subconscious mind? To do that, we must have some absolute standard of thinking and acting that will always be right, never wrong, and that we can rely upon 100% of the time. Where are we going to get that? I know of only one place to obtain such a reliable standard, and that is in the Bible's instructions for living. Before I became a Christian, I realized that in practicing psychiatry, everything that I was telling people that produced mental and emotional healing was somehow consistent with what Christ said to do in daily living. I was teaching people to forgive their parents for whatever rejection and abuse they had received from them. I urged patients to forgive other people who were hurting them in the present. I was seeing depressions healed, people learning to demonstrate courage rather than fear, people learning love rather than bitterness, and finding peace as a result. All those are things that Christ taught. I never saw anyone following His teachings and responding with despair. Instead, I saw that people who were rejecting Christ's teachings were producing loss of their mental health and damage to their lives and families.

Here we have a standard that is, in fact, reliable in producing mental health. The Bible's instructions for living will not only produce spiritual health, but will produce emotional health as well as physical health. For example, either spiritual or emotional turmoil may drive blood pressure up to dangerously high levels. High blood pressure may cause premature heart attacks, premature strokes, and thus premature disability or death. Spiritual and emotional turmoil may also produce gastritis, peptic ulcers, colitis, arthritis, headaches, and physical pain anywhere in the body.

It is quite important that adults as well as children understand that the purpose of authority is protection. The reason for being under parental authority is to benefit from the wisdom and protection of parents. A child who rejects parental authority and does the exact opposite of his parents' instructions and rules loses the benefit of parental protection. In the same way, a person who rejects God's authority loses the benefit of His protective rules and instructions, and suffers all of the consequences of not having that protection.

The phenomenon of identification has an important effect on the presence or absence of respect for authority. A child is not going to have respect for authority if he sees that his parents don't have it. If he sees his parents demonstrating scorn and contempt for their own parents, their government, employers, and ministers, the child is going to identify with that attitude and reproduce it. He is going to identify with what he sees the parents doing rather than what the parents instruct him to do. A parent who fails to demonstrate respect for authority is thus likely to see his children demonstrate that same disrespect, even for parental authority.

This is summarized very well in the Book of Deuteronomy, in Chapter 11, Verses 18 through 21 regarding God's commandments to the Jews (Good News Bible). *"Remember these commands and cherish them. Tie them on your arms and wear them on your foreheads as a reminder. 19 - Teach them to your children. Talk about them when you are at home and when you are away, when you are resting and when you are working. 20 - Write them on the doorposts of your houses and on your gates. 21 - Then you and your children will live a long time in the land that the Lord your God promised to give to your ancestors. You will live there as long as there is a sky above the earth."*

It is very interesting that here in Deuteronomy, the Bible gives instructions to follow God's commandments and to teach children to do likewise. This is followed by a promise that if that is done, both the adults and the children will have long lives. Following God's instructions for living is likely to increase one's lifespan by decreasing his level of stress. By following these instructions for living, one can avoid many disasters in living that would otherwise occur: marital disaster, disasters in emotional, spiritual, and physical health,

162

financial disaster, and social disaster. The Bible's teaching on finance (Proverbs 22:7, *"The borrower is servant to the lender."*) can prevent us from incurring debts that cause emotional stress. The Bible's rules for relating to other people can keep us out of chronic turmoil in our relationships. As we avoid emotional turmoil and stress, we also avoid many psychosomatic illnesses, such as high blood pressure, premature heart attacks, premature strokes, and often premature death. Deuteronomy, Chapter 11 thus gives both an instruction and a promise for obtaining a good life for ourselves as well as for our children.

Conclusion

Following these principles of parenting provides a foundation for the life and character of Jesus Christ to begin, grow, and become reflected in the lives of our children. Children do not usually see the person of Christ in this lifetime. Rather, they see the love of Christ reflected to them through the communication of love from parents. They learn to see, love, and reflect the character of Christ by seeing that character reflected by the lives of their parents. They learn to love and respect the authority of God by being taught to respect parents whose respect for God produces lives of peace, joy, and effectiveness for the parents as well as for their children.

Section Three:
Successful Christian Relationship
To Oneself

10

Developing Successful
Christian Self Image

Self image! What is it all about? It is obviously a problem which each of us faces. Emil Coue was a famous French psychotherapist of the late nineteenth century. Coue proposed an important yet frightening principle of the mind. He said that when the imagination and the will come into conflict, the imagination always wins! That's another way of saying that we may become what we believe or focus our minds upon. For example, a person who continually imagines himself to be sick may tell himself, "Each day, I am getting sicker and sicker." Sure enough, he is likely to do just that. Coue's solution to this problem was to teach people to control the imagination by taking charge of it. He gave his clients rosary-like beads to say daily; but rather than saying prayers with them, they were instructed to repeat therapeutic suggestions. For example, a hypochondriacal person would be taught to replace his suggestions of getting sicker each day with, "Each day, in every way, I am getting better and better." With each bead, he would repeat, "Each day, in every way, I am getting better and better." His mind would gradually become so saturated with this thought, that this became the predominant thought in his mind. His health was then quite likely to conform to his own suggestions.

The Bible has some very important things to say about the imagination. When the flood waters began to subside, Noah and his family got out of the ark on Mount Ararat in present-day Turkey. He built an altar and prepared a sacrifice to the Lord. Genesis 8:21 says, *"And the Lord smelled a sweet savour; and the Lord said in his heart, I will not again curse the ground any more for man's sake; for the imagination of man's heart is evil from his youth."* The Bible's references to the heart accurately describe the subconscious mind. This one indicates that if we indiscriminately permit our subconscious minds to determine our attitudes, especially our attitudes about ourselves, we are in trouble.

The most important aspect of self image is that it is the product of decision. Each day, we mentally talk to ourselves throughout the day. We make decisions about what kinds of things we say to ourselves. We tell ourselves positive or negative things, healthy or unhealthy things, truths or lies. We may tell ourselves throughout the day that we are inferior, or that we are like helpless children in the face of stress, or that we must be inadequate because a parent habitually acted inadequate. On the other hand, we may habitually tell ourselves things such as, "I am a capable, effective adult who can do whatever is the best thing." Or, "I can do all things through Christ who strengthens me." The concept that self image is the result of decision is very important, because if we have been damaging our self images with negative suggestions to ourselves, we can decide to replace those suggestions with new daily statements to ourselves. We can decide what we are going to silently or verbally say to ourselves about ourselves, our values, abilities, and potentials. Throughout my practice of psychiatry, I have seen people changing the troubled aspects of their self images by decision!

Reproducing The Character Of Christ

The Bible has some very important things to say about self image. The ideal self image — the self image that God wants us to have — is a reproduction of the character of Christ

168

(John 13:15, Ro. 15:5). Most of us are quite familiar with what the character of Christ is. He demonstrated love, courage, compassion, forgiveness, and a constant readiness to do whatever God the Father wanted Him to do. He led a very productive earthly life.

1 Peter 2:21 teaches, *"For even hereunto were ye called: because Christ also suffered for us, leaving us an example, that ye should follow his steps."*

Romans 8:29 tells us, *"For whom he did foreknow, he also did predestinate to be conformed to the image of his Son, that he might be the firstborn among many brethren."*

Phillipians 2:5 tells us, *"Let this mind be in you, which was also in Christ Jesus."* Here we are clearly given the concept that we should have a mind that copies the mind of Christ in as many ways as possible.

There does not seem to be an abundance of people demonstrating the character of Christ in their self images, nor many who have self images with which they themselves are satisfied. An important question becomes, "What wrecks the self image that Christ wants us to have?" Six major categories of self image wreckers interfere with our receiving the best that Christ wants to give us in this life.

SELF IMAGE WRECKER NO. 1
Acceptance Of Negative Parental Suggestions

One thing that wrecks this self image that Christ wants to give each of us is the individual's acceptance of negative words and suggestions that parents uttered during one's childhood, rather than accepting the word of God regarding oneself. Children are in a state of perpetual hypnosis in relationship to their parents. It is almost as if the parents are the first gods in a child's life, from infancy through the first five to seven years. These are the most important developmental years of the child's life. The child looks to the parents as examples and as people who know everything. As you look back on your own early childhood, you can remember how fantastic it seemed that your parents could do so many difficult things. It was impossible to even imagine how you could ever learn all of those things that they did.

As a child sees parents doing so many complex things, he begins to feel that the parents are always right, because they are right about so many things. This is a line of reasoning that even adults sometimes use in accepting the words of authorities. If authority figures are right about 90% of the things they say, most adults assume that those authorities must be right about everything. If a parent has said things to a child that are identical with the word of God regarding what one should be and say and do in given situations, there is no problem. It is in those areas in which what a parent has said is at variance with what God has said that a problem occurs. For example, a parent may have a self image defect in some area, such as in doubting his or her own ability to assume responsibility. The parent then similarly misperceives the child. The parent may communicate to the child that the child isn't expected to be capable of fulfilling responsibility. Every time an occasion arises in which the child should be assuming responsibility, such a parent takes over and does everything for the child. This pattern may get repeated over and over. The child should be walking down the block to play with the neighbors two houses down, and the parent is walking the child over there at six or seven years of age. The parent may demonstrate extreme anxiety every time the child is out of that parent's sight. Whenever the parent behaves in this way, he or she communicates to the child, "I don't believe that you are capable of being responsible. I don't believe that you are capable of taking care of yourself. I don't believe that you are capable of doing what an individual your age should be doing." A parent can thus subconsciously teach a child to think poorly of himself, to have a bad self image.

A parent may have a character defect in the area of honesty. Perhaps the parent had a tendency to steal during childhood, and never solidly built honesty into his character. That parent may expect the child to steal, even though the child may have never engaged in stealing. The parent repetitively questions him as though the parent believes that he has stolen things. As this continues, the subconsciously communicated message becomes, "I expect you to be a thief. I expect you to be dishonest. I expect you to have bad character in this area of living."

A parent may have some character defects in the area of sexual behavior, manifested by a history of adultery or premarital promiscuity. It could happen with either sex, but let us consider the example of a mother and her teenage daughter. This particular mother may be continually tempted to get involved in improper sexual relationships, but usually doesn't do it. She may inhibit this tendency because of religious belief, or for fear of damaging her marriage and losing her husband. Such a mother may subconsciously wish to obtain vicarious gratification from identifying with sexual promiscuity on the part of her virgin daughter. The mother consequently begins to question the daughter every time the daughter gets back from a date, as follows: "Alright, I know you were up to something in that car. What was going on? You might as well tell me." Meanwhile, there was no reality reason for the mother's reactions. The message thus communicated subconsciously by that mother is, "I want and expect you to be promiscuous." After dozens or even hundreds of such encounters, the child often begins obeying the parent's bizarre, subconscious suggestions and wishes.

There is obviously no limit to the areas of life in which parental character defects can get communicated to the child through this tremendous power of suggestion. Children are extremely sensitive to whatever parents expect of them. This is one of the most powerful forces of parental guidance. What the parent really expects the child to be and to do are thus communicated subconsciously as well as consciously.

Acceptance of such negative parental suggestions obviously wrecks the self images of children. Fortunately, this problem can be resolved. If you are having a particular problem with self image, such as feeling inadequate, or no

171

good, or incapable, this kind of message may have been communicated to you by a parent. You may be able to identify what happened as you review your life history. Once you identify this, you can say, "Alright. I can see what the problem is. I have accepted an erroneous suggestion from my parent. I reject that suggestion. Just as I accepted that error in the past, I can now reject it, by decision." Thereafter, each time negative thoughts arise, such as, "I'm inadequate, I'm no good, I'll never amount to anything," or whatever, you can then begin saying, "There it is again. I reject that suggestion. I am a capable, reliable adult who can do whatever is best and whatever I must." By identifying and rejecting negative parental suggestions, you can bring your attitude toward yourself into agreement with Christ's love for you. You can then accept His promises of peace, joy, and fruitfulness in your daily life.

Another way of overcoming previously accepted negative suggestions is through Christ-directed life, which can short-circuit them. An individual who is pressured by this kind of negative thinking may become a Christian and consecrate his life to Christ. It is essential that one not only make a "profession of faith," but also make a consecration of his life to the Lord. To get the best that Christ wants to give to us though Christian conversion, one should adopt the attitude, "Whatever Christ teaches is what I am going to think, say, and do. What I want is not as important as what Christ wants for me and of me." You can short circuit all negative thinking by means of a thorough dedication of every aspect of your life to the Lord. People who have been under the dominion of alcoholism, drug addiction, and all sorts of other moral, spiritual, or psychological problems have become suddenly healed when they made a real decision to dedicate their lives to Christ. Following Christ's instructions for living frees one from the control of the subconscious mind's lies or conflicts. In **Jeremiah 17:9,** we are told, *"The heart is deceitful above all things, and desperately wicked: who can know it?"* Whenever you experience a poor self image, it is always because of some subconscious lie. Lies such as "I must follow the negative suggestions of parents rather than the positive suggestions of Christ." Lies such as, "I must reproduce negative parental qualities rather than reproducing the character of Christ." You can reject those subconscious mind lies, and simply say, "What I want is not important. From now on, the character of Christ is going to be showing through me, rather than the old me."

SELF IMAGE WRECKER NO. 2
Negative Identification

A second image wrecker that can rob us of what Christ wants to give us, is identification with parental character defects, rather than identification with the character of Christ. Identification is a very powerful influence in the development of a child's emotional life and attitudes. Every child has a strong desire to be what he observes his parents to be. The behavioral instructions which he receives from his parents are important. But what parents say to a child is not nearly as influential as what they are in the child's presence. This has a tremendous influence upon every one of us.

I am convinced that 100% of people have a tug of war going on in their lives regarding parental character defects. Even if we have made conscious decisions to reject some character defects which parents had, we struggle with subconscious tendencies or temptations to reproduce that defect in our own lives. The battle between conscious efforts to reject the reproduction of parental character defects versus the subconscious tendency to demonstrate such defects is often disguised. Perhaps during a man's childhood, he often saw his father come home drunk, wreck the house, and beat the wife and children. The father tended to get drunk every night. The son resolves from childhood, "I'll never be an alcoholic like my father!" In adult life, this son may end up in a psychiatrist's office, suffering from depression, suicidal tendencies, and other problems which he has created for his

173

life by drinking too much alcohol. When the psychiatrist asks the man about his family background, he says, "Well, my father was an alcoholic. I made a vow that I'd never be an alcoholic, and I'm really glad that I'm not." The psychiatrist asks, "But what about all this drinking that you do?" The reply, "Oh, I'm not an alcoholic, because I don't drink every night, you see." This is a common story among alcoholics. Such a man has trained himself to lie to himself and believe it. "I'm not an alcoholic because I don't drink **every** night." Or, "I'm not an alcoholic because I can go for a month without touching any alcohol **if** I really want to. Ten years ago I quit drinking for one month, so that proves I'm not an alcoholic." Or, "I'm not an alcoholic, because I don't go home and wreck the house and lose control of myself. I can handle my drinking. How much do I drink? Oh, I guess six to ten a night, more on week-ends." Meanwhile, the individual has been progressively wrecking his life. One can observe many, subconscious, self-deceitful mechanisms by which such a man copies his father's disastrous problems. Others who did not have alcoholic parents may struggle against reproducing their parents' chronic anxiety, depression, dishonesty, adultery, disrespect for the opposite sex, or self contempt.

A helpful approach to overcoming emotional problems is to make a list of all the character or personality defects that you have ever seen each parent demonstrate. Then, conduct a careful survey of your life in search of identical problems or tendencies. If possible, get some objective person to assist in this comparison: perhaps your spouse, if you have a good relationship with that spouse, or a friend. As you identify those areas in which the problems of your parents' characters and personalities are being reproduced in your own life, you can then resolve to be different in those troubled areas.

Once these unhealthy, unsuccessful identifications are recognized, you can begin saying to yourself, "There it is. I have unwittingly copied my parent's emotional problem, or character defect. I am going to reject that, and replace it with the character that Christ demonstrated in that area." When we look for Christ's character, it shines toward us through those parental character defects. We can, if we wish, say to ourselves, "I love my parents, and they had some strengths that have been an asset to me. But that parental character defect that I see is in opposition to Christ's character. I am therefore going to use that parental character defect to show me the consequences of living in rejection of Christ's principles and character. I'm going to benefit from the difficult experiences of my parent. I can see what my parent lost and suffered as a result of that character defect. I don't need all that pain. I am simply going to use my familiarity with my parent's problem as free experience which God has provided me so that I won't have to make those painful errors."

We can use the character strengths as well as the character weaknesses of our parents in order to build character in ourselves. We can align our own character strengths with those of parents in each area in which the characters of our parents have reproduced Christ's character. We will then have no problem in those areas.

I once counselled a young woman who was suffering the consequences of severe alcoholism. She refused to admit to herself that she had a drinking problem. As the history of her life unfolded, she told me that her father had a very severe, damaging history of alcoholism. When I reviewed her spiritual life with her, she stated that she was agnostic. I asked her the reason for her doubts. She said, "When I was small, I saw all the destructiveness going on as a result of my father's drinking, and I prayed to God that he would be healed. He got healed several years later, but our family went through all of those years of pain as a result of his drunkenness. I felt that either God didn't answer my prayer, or that He wasn't there." She had made numerous attempts to take her life in the midst of drinking, with the alcohol chemically causing and intensifying depression.

I told her that there was another way to look at what

happened. A great deal of psychiatric research has provided evidence that a tendency to get into difficulty with alcohol may be genetically transmitted; that is, it may be a hereditary problem. I urged her to consider that God may have had something different in mind for her as a result of those experiences. God, being able to see the future, no doubt knew all about her genetic makeup, and that she would have a temptation to abuse alcohol. Perhaps God was giving her a clear opportunity to see the tragedy of not being totally abstinent when one has that kind of problem. It might be that God let that father's alcoholism continue for several additional years for her instruction regarding the tragic problems that would result from her own use of alcohol. Perhaps God wanted her to stay away from it completely, as many children of alcoholics do.

It was also significant to see that God actually did answer her prayer, but not at the instant that she wanted it answered. There was also some reason to suspect that God had been trying to reach out to that father, but he had kept saying, "No, I won't have you, Chirst. No, I won't have it your way." Her father had been rejecting what God wanted to give him. He consequently had to have more tragedy before he would give up his own futile ways and begin to receive the good life that God wanted to give to him.

When one looks objectively at another person's life, it is often easy to see the way that the Lord is trying to use such parental character defects to build character in the children. God would give children that free experience without their having to do such damaging things to themselves to learn how **not** to live. It is altogether too common for people to become embittered because God didn't do things their way at the very moment that they demanded. They then totally refuse to look at what God is trying to give them, which is often far more valuable than what they were requesting.

SELF IMAGE WRECKER NO. 3
Failing Because Of Parents

A third self image wrecker is a sense of failure or

inadequacy that results from bitterness towards parents because they were rejecting during one's childhood. Rather than the individual copying the strength, fruitfulness, and courage of the life of Christ, he chooses to demonstrate failure and inadequacy as a way of retaliating against parents who have hurt him. Anger towards parents is the most common reason that children fail in school. In such cases, parents have usually communicated rejection, or lack of love and concern to that child. The child who begins failing in the face of parental rejection usually becomes an adult who is continually tempted to fail so as to let down the parent who hurt him. But that wish to fail becomes disguised. It is unusual for such a person to admit to himself that he feels as follows: "I really want to mess up my job." Or, "I want to mess up my family life." Or, "I want to mess up my personal life, because I am so bitter and so unforgiving toward one or both of my parents." Rather than admit one's wish to fail to oneself, there is a tendency to disguise it, to deny the truth to oneself. More lies from the subconscious! One denies his true feelings and becomes totally unaware of what he is really doing. He is then left only with the feeling, "I can't do it. I can't handle the promotion that I just received." Or, "I can't handle the well paying, nice job that I have." Or, "I can't handle the great family life that God has given to me." Or, "I am simply too inadequate. I feel like such a failure." All of these attitudes may manifest bitterness towards parents, by means of a wish to fail or to create trouble for one's life. This robs one of what Christ really wants to give him regarding self image, or success.

SELF IMAGE WRECKER NO. 4
Fear of Being Imperfect

A fourth self image wrecker that will rob us of the tremendous self image and character that Christ wants to give us, is a fear of being imperfect. This is a particular problem when one has been parented by extreme perfectionists. I am not talking about ordinary parental discipline, in which the parent is trying to bring the child up in a proper manner. I am likewise not talking about excellence. I am talking about irrational perfectionism. I am talking about a parent who continually communicates to the child that nothing the child does will really be good enough! There will always be something wrong with anything which that child does, as far as that parent is concerned. This is the kind of perfectionism that can and does wreck self image.

An individual who had that kind of parenting demonstrates one of several responses. One is a depressed response, in which the individual says to himself, "I can't be perfect, no matter what I do. I am therefore simply no good, and I can never be any good. I'll keep trying, but I know that I'll never be adequate." Such an individual may be immensely successful. He may be a multi-millionaire. He may have tremendous position in his community or in his profession, or in his vocation. Down deep, however, he nonetheless feels inadequate. Consequently, he feels depressed, perhaps to the point of despair, because of his feeling, "I can never be O.K., because I can never be perfect."

A combination of things produces a bad result here. One is the failure to recognize that parental character defect which confronted the individual in childhood. One may fail to recognize that the parent was using criticism of the child as a demonstration of hositility and bitterness. One may fail to understand that his parent was sinning against him, rather than providing a realistic evaluation or constructive instruction. One then has tendency to take the parent's negative word for what he is, rather than accepting God's loving word. A second part of this problem is a failure to recognize that God is the only perfect being anyway, and that it is part of the human condition to be imperfect. There is likely to be occasional error in our performance, even if we are conscientious.

If we do a great many things, we are going to periodically

make an error. A man who is deathly afraid that he will make a grammatical error in a speech will probably never give a speech, because of fear. A person who never feels that he is functioning well enough, develops the attitude, "I'd better avoid this. I'd better avoid that. If I accept the responsibility to do those things, I may make a mistake, and that would be so awful that I couldn't face it." Such an individual continually avoids function because of an "inadequate" self image. **Inadequate** means never being adequately perfect to win the approval and affection of a parent.

A child who has been chronically criticized by a parent for not being perfect usually becomes embittered. No matter how hard he tries, he can never be "good enough" to receive the love and approval he desired from that parent. He may eventually stop trying to win the unavailable approval, and begin expressing his bitterness by failing, in order to frustrate or hurt the parent. He thereafter demonstrates a chronic tendency to fail because of his parent, rather than succeeding because of himself. Such an over-critical parent demonstrates disguised bitterness or hatred toward the child. This is usually the result of the parent's own self contempt being mentally projected onto the child, who is then seen as never being good enough.

SELF IMAGE WRECKER NO. 5
Subconsciously Assuming The Responsibility Of God

A fifth self image wrecker that can rob us of the self image that the Lord wants to give to us, is the subconscious assumption of the responsibility of God. This is a spiritual problem, but it causes the emotional problem of chronic anxiety.

A person who is failing to recognize the sovereignty of God throughout every aspect of his daily life tends to assume too much responsibility. He assumes responsibility for things totally beyond his control. Such an individual may be the

150th ranked person down from the top in a large corporation. He nonetheless becomes a nervous wreck, because the corporation is losing money. Whenever he sees top management making some mistake, he may becme bitter, depressed, and anxious about it. He feels that he must do something to change that situation, even though he doesn't have the power or the authority to do so. An individual may subconsciously assume the responsibility of God in relating to members of his family. At dinner in a restaurant, his spouse may make some error regarding the proper use of the eating utensils, or she may say something improper to the waiter. The individual may then experience a panic due to the feeling that he is responsible for his wife's behavior. He may even jeopardize his marriage, because he feels as if he must control everyone and everything about him.

A child may make some social error at a public function. The parent with this hangup may become intolerably embarrassed. He thinks, "What will my friends think of me, now that my child made this error?" He literally becomes a nervous wreck, merely because he is assuming the responsibility of God in feeling that he must control so much. If someone around him becomes physically ill, he feels that he must do something about it, although he may in reality be unable to do anything about it. It is totally beyond his control. One of the partners in a marriage may be experiencing severe emotional difficulties, such as severe anxiety, depression, or fear. That individual's spouse may feel that he must control this situation, take charge of it, solve it, somehow fix it. But he can't, because he can't get inside the mind of the spouse to fix the problem. This often causes both members of a marriage to lose their mental health.

This problem may reveal itself in the form of a severely over-developed self will. An individual who feels that he must control everything often becomes an extremely unpleasant person in the presence of other people. A person who subconsciously feels that he must carry out God's

180

responsibility makes others feel that he is trying to "take them over." So long as one is in the presence of such a person, one must do everything that person's way, or else trouble will erupt in the relationship. This often causes marital problems. It also causes an individual to be unable to conform to corporate working conditions. He may find himself unable to stay within the boundaries of the administrative authority of his position. He may try to overrule the authority of supervisors, often unwisely. Subconsciously feeling that one has to be God, rather than giving God the sovereignty, may thus cause severe damage to one's self image, emotional health, and all aspects of one's life.

SELF IMAGE WRECKER NO. 6
Theological Errors

Another category of self image wreckers that would deprive us of the self image that Christ wants us to have is the problem of theological errors.

Crucified With Christ?

The Bible teaches us that we are to be crucified with Christ **(Galatians 2:20, 5:24, 6:14).** There is a great deal of misunderstanding about what that means. One sometimes sees people crucifying their peace, joy, fruitfulness, relationships, and everything else that God is trying to give to them. They erroneously think that this is what it means to be a Christian: to go around being crucified all the time. This is not what it means to be a Christian. Being crucified with Christ means that we are to crucify our old selves, which have been run by our treacherous subconscious minds. We are to crucify our old character defects, and all of the resulting tendencies to mess up our lives. We need to die to the self will, and recognize that Christ has come to live in our spirits and direct our lives at the time we decided to accept Him as

181

our savior and Lord. We should let the character of Christ show through our thoughts, words, and actions. We then become resurrected in His Holy Spirit, and we begin to experience the peace, joy, and fruitfulness, which the Bible promises for Christ directed living.

Was Christ Weak?

There is a common tendency for people to erroneously think of Christ as a weak person, and to feel that in order to be Christ-like, one must be some kind of weakling, sissy, or an unhealthy individual. But this is not at all the picture that the Scriptures give us of Jesus Christ.

John, Chapter 18, Verses 4 through 6, teaches us, *"Jesus therefore, knowing all things that should come upon him, went forth, and said unto them, Whom seek ye? 5 - They answered him, Jesus of Nazareth. Jesus saith unto them, I am He. And Judas also, which betrayed him, stood with them. 6 - As soon then as he had said unto them, I am He, they went backward, and fell to the ground."* We get a glimpse there of the power which Christ had available against His adversaries when He chose to use that power.

In Luke, Chapter 4, Verses 28 to 30, the Bible says, *"And all they in the synagogue, when they heard these things, were filled with wrath, 29 - And rose up, and thrust him out of the city, and led him unto the brow of the hill whereon their city was built, that they might cast him down headlong. 30 - But he passing through the midst of them went his way."* Here we see Christ passing unharmed right through the middle of the very crowd that was trying to throw him over the cliff.

In Matthew 21:12-13, the Bible describes Jesus physically casting the money changers out of the temple and overturning their tables because of their cheating the worshippers out of money. This was not the behavior of a physically or emotionally weak man. Rather, it was the action of one who had the courage to act upon His spiritual and moral convictions. The other rabbis had apparently permitted such thievery to become a traditional part of the temple.

The strength of Christ is also illustrated in His portrayal of capability and productivity. In John 21:25, John writes of Jesus, *"And there are also many other things which Jesus did, the which, if they should be written every one, I suppose that even the world itself could not contain the books that should be written. Amen."*

A Promise of Happiness

In John, Chapter 13, Verses 14 through 17, Christ said, *"If I then, your Lord and Master, have washed your feet; ye also ought to wash one another's feet. 15 - For I have given you an example, that ye should do as I have done to you. 16 - Verily, verily, I say unto you, The servant is not greater than his Lord; neither he that is sent greater than he that sent him. 17 - If ye know these things, happy are ye if ye do them."*

Not only does Christ give us an example of what we should be; he also follows that example with the promise of happiness to those who would follow that example.

11

Outsmarting The Subconscious Mind With Christ Directed Living

The Bible makes the astounding statement that Christ refused to live according to His self will. John, in Chapter 8, Verses 28 and 29 says, *"Then said Jesus unto them, When ye have lifted up the Son of man, then shall ye know that I am he, and that I do nothing of myself; but as my Father hath taught me, I speak these things. 29 - And he that sent me is with me: the Father hath not left me alone; for I do always those things that please him."* In John, Chapter 5, Verse 30, we get the same message when Christ says, *"I can of mine own self do nothing: as I hear, I judge: and my judgment is just; because I seek not mine own will, but the will of the Father which hath sent me."* The Messiah Himself would thus not run His life by self will.

I would like to emphasize three concepts about the subconscious mind. First, the subconscious mind is so treacherous that it is impossible for anyone to direct his life with his own self will without periodically shipwrecking his life through his subconscious motivations and conflicts. The second concept is that the subconscious mind is basically evil in its effects and in its contents. The third is that Christ-directed living is the only way that one can reliably short-circuit the subconscious mind and remove its obstruction to peaceful, joyful, fruitful living.

The Subconscious Makes It Impossible For
Anyone To Direct His Own Life

In Jeremiah 10:23, the Bible teaches, *"O Lord, I know that the way of man is not in himself: it is not in man that walketh to direct his steps."* In the 17th Chapter of Jeremiah, Verses 9 and 10, the prophet says, *"The heart is deceitful above all things, and desperately wicked: who can know it? 10 - I the Lord search the heart, I try the reins, even to give every man according to his ways, and according to the fruits of his doing."*

Those are remarkable statements. Taken together, they communicate that no one can really direct his own life, apparently because the heart of man is so deceitful that we cannot know what is in our own minds. I gather from these Scriptures that the heart of man is even more deceitful than Satan. The Bible says that it is deceitful above **all** things. The Bible's descriptions of the heart are characteristics of what we now call the subconscious mind.

The Subconscious Causes Conflict

The functioning of the subconscious is one of the most perplexing phenomena imaginable. For example, it is very common that we subconsciously want to do the opposite things from what we consciously desire. Hence, we have the phenomenon of conflict, which produces anxiety. A person may want to function and be successful at the same time that he wants to fail. He may subconsciously hold a grudge against his parents, who rejected him during his childhood, and he doesn't want them to obtain gratification from his success. Yet he wants to be successful. Whenever our subconscious wishes or feelings conflict with our conscious motivations, we experience the emotion of anxiety.

One may experience a conflict about expressing his wishes, feelings, or needs. He may consciously wish to express that he needs something from someone whom he loves. At the same time, experiences with childhood rejection may cause him to subconsciously feel that if he does express himself, he is only going to receive rejection. Whenever he needs affection from somebody, he is consequently in a state of conflict and anxiety, because he feels a strong desire both to express his need and to conceal it at the same time. It is not unusual for people to simultaneously love and hate the same person. They may have a natural inclination to consciously love people, but because of continuing bitterness about childhood rejection by their parents, they subconsciously hate anyone to whom they get close. It readily becomes apparent that the subconscious mind is crazy; it is absolutely insane! This is what each of us has between our ears. We have a crazy, subconscious mind that often feels and wants two opposite things at one time.

The Subconscious Is Systematically Illogical

Another characteristic of the subconscious mind is a phenomenon that is referred to as primary process thinking, or predicate thinking. This is a very illogical, unrealistic form of thinking. The subconscious mind tends to equate things that have only one characteristic in common. For example, "Mother was a woman. Mother emotionally injured me. My wife is a woman. Therefore my wife will emotionally injure me." Here you see a very unrealistic equating of things which have only one characteristic in common, in spite of a large number of differences. This subconscious equating of things that have only one characteristic in common causes a phenomenon referred to in psychiatry as **transference.** We transfer troubled, childhood feelings about our parents onto other people in our adult life. This obviously produces many problems for us.

The Subconscious Is Deceitful

Another characteristic of the subconscious mind gives us a glimpse of what the Bible is referring to when it describes the heart of man as being deceitful above all things. The phenomena of **denial** and **repression** demonstrate that the subconscious mind is a liar. In order to avoid anxiety, we lie to ourselves by denying or repressing the awareness of certain feelings and truths in our daily living. We begin doing this from an early age. For example, a person received severe parental rejection during childhood and felt hurt by it. He may have repressed the realization that a parent did this to him. He simply lied to himself through his subconscious, and said to himself, "That never really happened. My father never abused me, or rejected me." Or, "My mother never really demonstrated that she didn't care much about me." He becomes bitter about this rejection. The bitterness causes depression. But he represses the causes of the bitterness, thus having no conscious knowledge of why he is depressed! Psychiatrists often see people in middle age and old age who have been depressed all of their lives for some repressed reason such as this. Proverbs 28:26 tells us, *"He that trusteth in his own heart is a fool: but whoso walketh wisely, he shall be delivered."* Proverbs 21:2 says, *"Every way of a man is right in his own eyes: but the Lord pondereth the hearts."*

Here we get another glimpse of the phenomena of denial and repression. A person who has a strong inclination to do something that is wrongful may gradually begin telling himself all sorts of lies until he destroys his conscious awareness and judgment in that area. He may have a serious drinking problem, and he tells himself, "Well, this isn't all that bad. I only drink wine and beer rather than hard liquor. Besides, I could quit if I really decided to, so I'm not an alcoholic." A person may experience a compulsion to be unfaithful to his spouse. He will tell himself, "Well, adultery is not really that bad. This is a new era. The Scriptures were written a long time ago. Things have changed now. Besides, I'm not really hurting anyone." People have a tendency to deceive their conscious minds with this self deception of their own subconscious minds. Hebrews 3:12-13 tells us, *"Take heed, brethren, lest there be in any of you an evil heart of unbelief, in departing from the living God. 13 - But exhort one another daily, while it is called To day: lest any of you be hardened through the deceitfulness of sin."*

Here we begin to see a link between the deceitfulness of the subconscious, or the heart, and sin. We may commit some sin during childhood, such as becoming bitter and unforgiving toward a parent. Then we deny to ourselves that we are committing that sin. The bitterness becomes turned inward, and becomes depression, which may continue in adult life. An adult with such a chronic depression may tell himself, "I really loved my parents. I never had any ill feelings toward them at all." By not permitting himself to be convicted of his improper and harmful attitudes, the individual experiences chronic problems over many decades. Should he have permitted himself to be convicted, he could have confessed the sin, accepted Christ's forgiveness, forgiven his parents, and been healed.

The Subconscious Projects Our Own Feelings Unto Others

Another phenomenon that we frequently observe in the subconscious mind is called **projection,** or a tendency to subconsciously disown our own feelings and attribute them to others. For instance, an individual may have a tendency to feel such extreme bitterness towards another person, that he would really like to kill that person. He is full of rage. Maybe that person did something so vicious to him that he would be expected to feel that way, from a natural point of view. But the individual finds that these feelings are quite unacceptable to his conscience. In order to avoid the tremendous anxiety that he feels about his murderous rage, he may deny to himself that he really feels the rage. He then begins attributing these feelings to other people. He may especially attribute the wish to kill to the same person toward whom he feels the hatred. He then begins to think, "So and so is going to kill me!" This is the cause of a paranoid personality, in which paranoia dominates one's life. All of us may at times feel a little paranoid. We may feel that somebody is trying to hurt us when they really are not. When such paranoid feelings are analyzed, one may realize, "Well, I really had a lot of bitterness towards that individual, and I expected him to treat me the way I felt like treating him." Projection is thus something that anyone can experience at times. This is another glimpse of the subconscious mind's tremendous capacity for deceitfulness.

The Subconscious Turns Feelings Toward Others Upon Ourselves

Another trick that the subconscious mind likes to play on us is labeled **introjection,** in psychoanalytic theory. It means that we have a tendency to turn our feelings inward upon ourselves. For example, if we become extremely angry with someone else, we have a tendency to turn that anger towards ourselves. This results in depression. If we feel so angry with another person that we experience the wish to kill him, the subconscious mind has a tendency to turn that impulse inward upon ourselves. This produces the phenomenon of suicidal thoughts and behavior. Suicide is usually caused by a wish to kill someone turned inward upon the self. Psychiatric interviews of people who have made unsuccessful suicide attempts reveals the history that they were either extremely angry with someone right before they made the attempt, or chronically angry with rejecting, abusive parents since childhood.

The Subconscious Converts Emotions Into Physcial Symptoms

Proverbs 4:20-22 tell us, *"My son, attend to my words; incline thine ear unto my sayings. 21 - Let them not depart from thine eyes; keep them in the midst of thine heart. 22 - For they are life unto those that find them, and health to all*

189

their flesh.'' This proverb teaches that paying careful attention to the word of God and keeping it in our hearts will produce physical health. When one reads something like this, he is inclined to say to himself, "How can that be? How can keeping the word of God in my heart give me physical health?'' Following Christ's instructions for responding to each life situation is a reliable substitute for responding to life with subconscious mind directed activity, such as producing physical disorders. The subconscious mind tends to do something that has been labeled **conversion;** it converts feelings into physical experiences. For example, an individual who has a strong wish to injure someone with his right hand may repress that wish and develop psychological paralysis of the right hand. This solves his conflict about whether or not to injure the other person. It is now impossible to do this.

Another way that the subconscious mind converts emotion into physical symptoms is by means of headaches. Headaches are usually caused by anger. There are times when headaches can be caused by something physical, such as viruses or brain tumors, but most headaches are caused by anger. If you get a headache, pause for a moment, and begin asking yourself, "With whom am I angry?'' You will almost always realize that shortly before that headache began, you were very angry with someone. Realizing this will usually eliminate the headache, especially if you resolve the anger by forgiveness of that person. All sorts of pain syndromes can be caused by emotion being converted into something physical. Back pains and arthritis are often caused by depression. A person who is chronically depressed, or angry, or anxious, may secrete excessive hydrochloric acid in the stomach and develop peptic ulcers. A woman with negative feelings about her femininity may experience severe physical pain with menstrual periods. A housewife may feel that an invalid parent is making excessive demands upon her for nursing care. The woman may feel a conflict between burden and guilt. She may experience a minor backstrain which would normally heal in twenty-four hours. However, she goes to bed for one day and discovers that this is an excellent solution to the burdening demands of her invalid parent. She is no longer expected to nurse the parent, and since she too is now sick, she does not feel guilty about this. However, she must be in pain to justify not taking care of that parent. The subconscious comes to her rescue. It begins generating physical back pain in order to relieve the emotional pain of her anxiety and depression due to the conflict about caring for the parent. The woman's refusal to be truthful with herself about her feelings prevents her from finding acceptable reality solutions to her situation. Instead, she solves it by becoming a chronic invalid from back pain.

Love and Forgiveness Heal Both Body and Mind

Saturating the conscious as well as the subconscious mind with the word of God can solve or prevent emotional problems. For example, if you get angry with someone, what are you going to do? You can go to the Bible and say to yourself, "Christ said to forgive this person, and to actually pray for him." Following Christ's instructions will have the effect of destroying your headache, or your depression, or your ulcers, or your psychosomatic joint pains. Perhaps a boss or a spouse has mistreated you. This can be successfully dealt with by a decision to act on love and forgiveness. You might say to yourself, "This individual mistreated me, but he is a human being. He has more than his share of problems, but look at my problems. He is probably not much worse off than I am. Part of the human condition is that no one is perfect. It just so happens that I got some of the flack from that person's problems, because I happened to be in that position at that time. I can give some consideration to this person. I can see some of his human problems. He will simply have to deal with those problems. I was just inconvenienced, that's all." This type of attitude utilizes the love that Christ taught. You can thus destroy physical symptoms that have been caused by failure to demonstrate loving, forgiving attitudes toward someone close to you.

The Subconscious Is Evil

The Bible teaches that the subconscious mind is evil in its contents. In Matthew Chapter 15, Verses 18 and 19, Jesus said, *"But those things which proceed out of the mouth come forth from the heart; and they defile the man. 19 - For out of the heart proceed evil thoughts, murders, adulteries, fornications, thefts, false witness, blastphemies."* Christ is not saying, **"Some** of you have hearts containing these things."** He is making a generalized statement. It may seem hard to imagine that everyone would have things like murder, adultery, or fornication in his own heart, as a normal part of the human condition. Yet, observation of the subconscious mind reveals the existence of a phenomenon which has been labeled the **Oedipus complex.** Freud discovered that during psychological development, between the ages of four and seven years, people experience a wish to have the parent of the opposite sex all to themselves. They subconsciously wish that they could get rid of the parent of the same sex. Then they could receive all of the affection that the parent of the opposite sex has to give. In the phenomenon of the Oedipus complex, one can see the truth of Christ's teaching in Matthew 15:18-19. There is murder, and there is adultery in everyone's heart. In addition, the subconscious mind may interpret anger toward someone as a wish to kill that person. We may dream that someone who angered us the previous day has been killed in an accident. Such dreams are often pressured by a subconscious wish.

It is not unusual for repressed, subconscious feelings from the oedipal years of childhood to cause adults to compulsively commit adultery. For example, a little girl's father may desert the family to be with another woman. That little girl may then say to herself, "I have to get my daddy back, no matter what. Someday, I am going to take him away from that woman. Someday, I am going to get even with her for stealing my Daddy from me when I need him and love him so much." These thoughts are so painful that the child represses them, or buries them in her subconscious mind. As an adult woman, she subconsciously remembers that vow to "get back at the other woman." She then finds herself attracted exclusively to married men. Her subconscious motivation is merely to destroy a man's marriage, and to hurt both him and his wife. Her bitterness toward her father as well as the woman with whom he ran off is being transferred to the married man and his wife in the present. Once she succeeds in breaking up that marriage, she suddenly finds herself inexplicably losing interest in that man. She finally leaves him to pursue a relationship with some other married man. Here we see sex used merely for destructive purposes. I have seen many cases identical to this, caused by the repressed, evil intentions of the subconscious mind.

The false witness of which Jesus spoke in Matthew 15:19 may refer in part to the phenomena of denial and repression, in which we deny to ourselves what we really think and feel.

After the flood had begun to subside, and Noah offered a sacrifice to God, Genesis 8:21 tells us, *"And the Lord smelled a sweet savour; and the Lord said in his heart, I will not again curse the ground any more for man's sake; for the imagination of man's heart is evil from his youth; neither will I again smite any more every thing living, as I have done."* Here, near the beginning of the Bible, God is communicating to us that the imagination of man's heart is evil from his youth. God is not saying, "Some of you may have this kind of a heart." Instead, he is making a very general statement about the heart of each of us.

Solution: Christ-Directed Living

We thus come to the concept that the Christ-directed life is the only reliable means of really short-circuiting this subconscious mind and producing a good life for oneself. In John 14:21 Christ says, *"He that hath my commandments, and keepeth them, he it is that loveth me: and he that loveth me shall be loved of my Father, and I will love him, and will manifest myself to him."* Here we have a promise that if we follow Christ's teachings and laws, He will manifest Himself to us. Proverbs 3:5-6 promises further: *"Trust in the Lord with all thine heart; and lean not unto thine own understanding. 6 - In all thy ways acknowledge him, and he shall direct thy paths."*

Whatever We Give Up For Christ Is Returned

Whenever one is faced with the idea of using Christ's instructions as a way of living, rather than living by his own impulses or wishes, he often has to give up something. It is usually something that he knows really doesn't belong in his life. "How can I give up all of my sins to follow Christ?" is the inevitable question that each of us has to face. The answer is that whatever Christ wants to give us will ultimately be somehow better than the fruits of sinful behavior. We can use Christ-directed living to avoid shipwreck and to get those things that God wants to give us in this life. The greatest secret in the world is probably the realization that whatever God wants to give us is truly the best thing possible for our lives.

In Luke 18:22-30, Christ taught an important message when the rich young man refused to give up his riches to follow Him. The wealth was not the problem. The problem was that **this** man's wealth was the most important thing in his life. One can see this from his choice to leave Christ for the riches. It appears that Jesus looked into that man's heart and saw that his money was more important to him than was God. We know that Abraham was very wealthy. David was very wealthy. Solomon was very wealthy. That seemed to be no particular problem for those men. But for this particular rich young man, wealth was a snare to his relationship with God. For that reason, Christ wanted him to give up his wealth. *"For it is easier for a camel to go through a needle's eye, than for a rich man to enter into the kingdom of God (Luke 18:25)."*

194

In Luke 18:28-30, the Bible says, *"Then Peter said, Lo, we have left all and followed thee. 29 - And he said unto them, Verily I say unto you, there is no man that hath left house, or parents, or brethren, or wife, or children, for the kingdom of God's sake, 30 - Who shall not receive manifold more in this present time, and in the world to come life everlasting."* That is an incredible promise! Christ is promising that whenever we give up anything in this life to follow Him, we are going to receive many times more than that in **this present lifetime**. It is not merely a question of saying, "Well, if I give up this or that in order to follow Christ and His teachings, I'll get to Heaven. But what about my earthly life now and over the remaining decades of it?" Right here in this scriptural promise is the answer: anything that is given up is going to be returned "manifold more in this present time, and in the world to come, life everlasting."

Part of my personal testimony is that in the course of my Christian development, anything that I have given up to follow Christ was, in fact, restored manifold. Christ has kept this promise in my life. He gave me things of much more value than were all of those things that I ever gave up, which He didn't want in my life.

Obedience To God Produces Peace

In Colossians 3:15, the Bible says, *"And let the peace of God rule in your hearts, to the which also ye are called in one body; and be ye thankful."* This is a very important instruction: "Let the peace of God rule in your hearts." This means that if we are following God's instructions in any situation, He is going to give us peace. We may be facing a difficult situation which we know is going to be stressful. If we face it and handle it the way that Christ has instructed that we conduct ourselves in such a situation, we find that we have peace, in spite of tremendous reality difficulty. On the other hand, if we're facing something, and whenever we consider doing a particular thing, we feel anxiety or despair, it is often the result of our violating Christ's teachings. The conscience rebels. The peace in our hearts is lost by considering an unChristian solution to a problem. That means we must reconsider and find another solution which permits us to keep our peace. For example, an individual who is angry with his wife and is tempted to kill himself as a result, may become so depressed that he can no longer work, and becomes emotionally disabled. An individual who is merely toying around with an idea such as suicide experiences tremendous anxiety, because he knows that if he were to carry out his impulses, it would be disastrous.

Another individual may be having so much trouble with his boss, that he experiences a strong impulse to punch the boss in the face. He would really like to retaliate. He knows however, that if he does that, he will lose his job, and may have difficulty getting another job with that on his job record. He may get sued. He may kill or cripple the boss accidentally, or that may happen to him. He consequently experiences acute anxiety, which is the exact opposite of peace in his heart. The anxiety is a signal that God's peace has left his heart as a result of his having departed from Christ's instructions for responding to his situation.

We can use the peace that God promises us for following His instructions, as a guide in handling ourselves in difficult situations. If we feel ourselves losing our peace, we know that we had better take another look at our relationship with the Lord and his teachings at that moment.

The Bible contains many other promises of peace in return for following the teachings and instructions of Christ. A real snare for most people is their search for **happiness** rather than **peace.** They ask, "What will make me happy?" Then they get what they thought would make them happy. Shortly afterwards, they need something newer, or something bigger, or something more to make them happy. There is no end to seeking happiness, or seeking thrills. Yet, this is what many people seek. It is important to realize that happiness is not the thing to seek. What one really needs is peace, and when he has that, he is truly O.K.

Proverbs, 16:7 tells us, *"When a man's ways please the Lord, he maketh even his enemies to be at peace with him."* That is a tremendous promise. Psalm 119:165 tells us, *"Great peace have they which love thy law: and nothing shall offend them."* Again we have a promise of peace for following the Lord's ways.

The Bible contains other promises of God for peace in return for following His word. I would like to conclude with one of my favorite of God's promises, which is somewhat extensive. This is Luke, Chapter 6, Verses 46 to 49: *"And why call ye me, Lord, Lord, and do not the things which I say? 47 - Whosoever cometh to me, and heareth my sayings, and doeth them, I will shew you to whom he is like: 48 - He is like a man which built an house, and digged deep, and laid the foundation on a rock: and when the flood arose, the stream beat vehemently upon that house, and could not shake it: for it was founded upon a rock. 49 - But he that heareth, and doeth not, is like a man that without a foundation built an house upon the earth; against which the stream did beat vehemently, and immediately it fell; and the ruin of that house was great."*

Here we have promises both for following Christ's teachings and for rejecting them. My psychiatric work with a large number of people has taught me that those promises are always kept. It is very difficult to get very far in life without having moments of despair. If you will reflect upon those times when you were in despair, you will be able to identify at least one of Christ's teachings which were violated prior to the onset of that despair. Likewise, by reflecting upon the time that you pulled out of that despair, you can retrospectively identify some teaching of Christ that you began to make a part of your life just prior to that time. No matter what your external situation or circumstances may be, aligning your thoughts, words, and actions with the teachings of Christ will always turn your life around from despair to peace.

12

Pride, Masochism, and Humility In Christian Life

When is suffering a Christian thing to do, and when is it just plain masochism? When is self respect or self confidence a proper part of Christian life, and how does it differ from pride? When is being humble a proper part of Christian life, and how does it differ from being masochistic? These are important and often confusing matters to Christians as well as to non-Christians. Non-Christians sometimes question and even scorn Christian life as a result of common misunderstandings about these terms. Christians sometimes damage their witness and their mental health because of lack of understanding of the differences between pride, masochism, and humility.

Definitions

Pride is the expression of an over-developed self will, and is greatly discouraged by the Scriptures. The prideful person says to himself, "I'm going to do everything **my** way. Who is God that He should interfere? Who is anyone, that he should interfere with anything that I want? People should realize how important I am." The essence of this attitude is, "What I want is better and more important than what God wants for me."

Mental masochism is a self degrading attitude in which an

individual feels that he is too inferior to be an able servant of God, others, or himself. His self degrading attitude causes him to receive chronic damage at the hands of others as well as at his own hands, while he rejects or mentally devaluates many good things which God would like to give him. The masochistic person says, "No, God, I won't serve you, because I am not good enough. Furthermore, whatever I have is of little value."

Humility is the attitude of being humble toward God. The humble person feels that he can do whatever God wants him to do or gives him to do. The humble person is not one who grovels or acts lowly before others with the masochistic attitude, "Look how worthless I am." Neither does the humble person pridefully communicate, "Look how great I am." Rather, the humble person communicates self respect, knowing that he is a forgiven sinner whom God loves. He feels, "I can do all things through Christ, who strengthens me." Humility is the position that the Bible urges us to adopt.

Pride And Its Effects

It is very clear in the Scriptures that when the Lord looks at our hearts, He often sees something quite different from what we are willing to see in ourselves (1 Chronicles 28:9, Proverbs 21:2, Jeremiah 17:9-10). One of the things that He dislikes seeing in us is what the Bible calls **pride.** Pride is an attitude which involves placing our self will above the will of God for our lives. This results from failure to recognize that God is infinitely wiser than we are, and that whatever He wants for us is truly the best thing for our lives. The person who fails to recognize the love and wisdom in God's sovereignty over our lives is likely to rebel against God through the attitude of pride. Pride causes one to depart from Christ-directed living and to run his life on subconscious mind function. Pride led Moses, Paul, and even King David (who had Uriah killed) to commit murder.

199

The term **pride** must be distinguished from the concept of self respect. Self respect may be defined as an acknowledgement that God loves us and that we are His children once we accept Him as our Father and Christ as our savior. We must have a certain amount of self respect in order to accept the love of God or of others, and to love God and others. Without self respect, one inevitably experiences self contempt or self hate, which can disable one emotionally, spiritually, and even physically. When Christ was asked which is the most important commandment, he replied (Matthew 22:37-39) that we should love God and also *"love thy neighbour as thyself."*

Pride Causes Wickedness

Psalms 10:2-5 teaches, *"The wicked in his pride doth persecute the poor: let them be taken in the devices that they have imagined. 3 - For the wicked boasteth of his heart's desire, and blesseth the covetous, whom the Lord aborreth. 4 - The wicked, through the pride of his countenance, will not seek after God; God is not in all his thoughts. 5 - His ways are always grievous; thy judgements are far above out of his sight."*
Here in the 10th Psalm pride is linked to wickedness, to persecution of the poor, and to a disastrous refusal to seek after the Lord.
Malachi 4:1 also reveals that pride is associated with wickedness: *"For, behold, the day cometh, that shall burn as an oven; and all the proud, yea, all that do wickedly, shall be stubble: and the day that cometh shall burn them up, saith the Lord of Hosts, that it shall leave them neither root nor branch."*

Pride Causes Contention

Proverbs 13:10 tells us, *"Only by pride cometh contention: but the well advised is wisdom."* Proverbs 28:25 says, *"He that is of a proud heart stirreth up strife: but he that putteth his trust in the Lord shall be made fat.''* Both of these proverbs teach that a person who is very proud causes strife, or contention. Furthermore, Proverbs 13:10 makes the remarkable statement that **only** by pride comes contention. That's a very important statement. Apparently, it is impossible to have contention without pride. How can that be?

A person who is dominated by pride doesn't see anything but his own way, and his own will. He gets into conflicts with people because he is convinced that he is always right, no matter what his position may be. He is totally unable to consider the positions of other people. He is usually unable to see anything wrong in his own position, and unable to see anything right in anyone else's position when theirs differs from his own. Consequently, "Only by pride cometh contention," is a very important psychological and spiritual truth.

Pride Causes Alcoholism

Many of the truths which the Bible teaches us about alcoholism aren't even understood by most psychiatrists today. The Scriptures teach a surprising connection between alcoholism and pride. Isaiah 28:3 says, *"The crown of pride, the drunkards of Ephraim, shall be trodden under feet."* Ephraim was one of the largest and most successful tribes of Israel. The Book of Habakkuk, 2:4-5 says, *"Behold, his soul which is lifted up is not upright in him: but the just shall live by his faith. 5 - Yea also, because he transgresseth by wine, he is a proud man, neither keepeth at home, who enlargeth his desire as hell, and is as death, and cannot be satisfied, but gathereth unto him all nations, and keepeth unto him all people."* Here again, the Bible is linking the abuse of alcohol with pride.

Pride Causes Covetousness

In Habakkuk 2:9, the Bible says, *"Woe to him that*

201

coveteth an evil covetousness to his house, that he may set his nest on high, that he may be delivered from the power of evil!" Habakkuk associates pride with progressively troublesome things. First he talks about pride leading to the abuse of wine, and then he links pride with covetousness. Covetousness is a feeling that one must have some status of wealth, position, or power in order to be okay, without regard to the will or sovereignty of God.

Pride Causes Self Deception

Proverbs, 12:15 says, *"The way of a fool is right in his own eyes: but he that hearkeneth unto counsel is wise."* Here the Bible gives us a glimpse of the disastrous effects of trusting our own judgments apart from God. Our own judgments are always clouded by the subconscious mind. We get another indication of this in Proverbs 14:12. *"There is a way which seemeth right unto a man, but the end thereof are the ways of death."* It is alarming to consider what God is saying. It is easy for a man to think that he is doing right, while unwittingly heading for his destruction. Pride causes one to reject the wisdom and guidance of God. This leaves one directing his life by means of subconscious mind function. At that point, one's life is headed for inevitable disaster. Pride thus causes one's destruction. Obadiah 1:3-4 also links pride with self deception: *"**The pride of thine heart hath deceived thee,** thou that dwellest in the clefts of the rock, whose habitation is high; that sayeth in his heart, Who shall bring me down to the ground? 4 - Though thou exalt thyself as the eagle, and though thou set thy nest among the stars, thence will I bring thee down, saith the Lord."* Pride causes one to deceive himself even about the contents and motivations of his own mind.

The Self Deception of Pride Causes Spiritual Blindness

By causing one to be unable to see himself objectively,

202

pride produces spiritual blindness. In Exodus 5:2 when Moses and Aaron spoke to the Pharoah, the Bible says, *"And Pharoah said, Who is the Lord, that I should obey his voice to let Israel go? I know not the Lord, neither will I let Israel go."* Pharoah was the absolute ruler of Egypt. He revealed pride by his statement that he was unconcerned with God's will. This was probably the reason that God chose to harden Pharoah's heart. He had obviously lived his entire life with no concern for anything but his own will. Whenever the Bible says that God hardened someone's heart, it is someone who had previously demonstrated an enormous amount of pride, and who was thoroughly unconcerned with what the Lord wanted. God abandons to sin those who have an exaggerated self will. Such people end up with hardened hearts, because no matter what anyone says about God, they are totally unwilling to listen, or comprehend, or agree.

In Luke, Chapter 16, we are told about the encounter between Lazarus and Abraham in heaven, and the rich man in Hell. The rich man asked Abraham to permit Lazarus to rise from the dead to witness to his five brothers so that his brothers wouldn't end up in hell also. Verse 31 says of Abraham's reply, *"And he said unto him, If they hear not Moses and the prophets, neither will they be persuaded, though one rose from the dead."* Even observing someone arise from the dead is not sufficient to alter the stubborn opinions and spiritual blindness of people whose hearts have been hardened by pride.

In Ephesians 4:17-18, Paul writes, *"This I say therefore, and testify in the Lord, that ye henceforth walk not as other Gentiles walk, in the vanity of their mind. 18 - Having the understanding darkened, being alienated from the life of God through the ignorance that is in them, because of the blindness of their heart."* The understanding can thus be darkened by vanity of the mind. Regarding the subject of spiritual blindness, in Jeremiah 9:3, God says of the Jews, *"They proceed from evil to evil, and they know not me, saith the Lord."* In Jeremiah 9:6, God continues to describe the

Jews, *"Thine habitation is in the midst of deceit; through deceit they refuse to know me, saith the Lord."* Pride produces self deceit and causes people to fail to comprehend the Lord and what He wants. In Jeremiah 17:9-10, the Bible teaches, *"The heart is deceitful above all things, and desperately wicked: who can know it? 10 - I the Lord search the heart, I try the reins, even to give every man according to his ways, and according to the fruit of his doings."* This passage contains one of the most important truths in the Bible. The statement, "The heart is deceitful above all things and desperately wicked, who can know it?" is saying that even a psychiatrist cannot know everything that is in the heart of a man! While a psychiatrist can obtain glimpses of the subconscious mind, he can never see everything in it the way God can.

The problem of pride leading to spiritual blindness and hardened hearts is one of the reasons that many people do not receive a healing through psychiatric treatment. It is usually very easy for a capable psychiatrist to understand what is wrong with his patients, as well as how they got that way. It is easy for such a psychiatrist to point out what the individual must do to turn his life around and replace despair with peace. But if a person has a hardened heart, no one can verbally or mentally get through to him. Such a person may look at you while you're speaking to him, but he acts as though he won't really **hear** what you've got to say. He won't really respond in a reasonable manner, regardless of who is counselling him. In Exodus 5:2, Pharoah, whose heart had been hardened, responded to Moses, *"Who is the Lord, that I should obey his voice to let Israel go?"* This is the basic attitude of a person with a hardened heart. "Who is God that I should listen to Him?" "Who is my spouse that I should listen to her?" "Who is my doctor that I should listen to him?" "Who are my children that I should listen to them?" He won't listen to anyone, and this eventually produces disaster in his life. When I encounter a person with a hardened heart in my psychiatric consulting room, I know that I will never help that person unless God softens his heart and sends him back to me at a later time. Prior to such a time as that, that person would merely waste time and money in a psychiatrist's office. Consultations with such people have revealed to me that it is an attitude of pride which leads to their hardened hearts.

A prominent, successful business man was brought to my office one day by his grown son. The son had become fearful for his father's welfare because of the father's alcoholism and depression. This man was an important leader in his community. Yet, alcoholism was ruining his whole life. When treatment for his alcoholism was suggested and even urged not only by his family, but by me, his response was, "I can handle that myself. I'll be alright." Less than six months later, this individual died on his farm, where he did most of his drinking. He was operating a piece of farm equipment, fell, and was killed by that machine. It was quite likely that he had been drinking at the time. He would not listen to anyone. He was very intelligent, and yet it was obvious to everyone but him that he needed help. He was a proud man, and his heart was hardened to counsel.

Another man was running several business ventures simultaneously. He continually demanded complete control of everything around him. Though he had no training in medicine, whenever he received medical consultations, he would dictate the treatment to his doctors. He would give them lists of those medicines with which he wanted to be treated, lists of those which he refused. He dictated when he would be hospitalized, and for what length of time, what procedures he was to have, etc. He often rejected the recommendations of his physicians. He also made it a point to inform everyone he encountered of the amount of his annual income. He would often comment, "I'll bet **you** never made that amount of money." He made it a practice to loudly rebuke his wife in public places, and had often threatened to leave her over a period of several months. A short time after my initial contact with him, he became overtly psychotic, discovered that he was on the verge of bankruptcy, and learned that his wife wanted a divorce. This individual conducted a running battle with suicidal inclinations. The same pride which caused all of his other problems was causing him to refuse to forgive parental mistreatment and abuse of him during childhood. This refusal to forgive was causing a chronic, recurring depression and psychosis which periodically incapacitated him. His pride caused him to be unamenable to counsel, and deprived him of a cure.

Pride Causes Deterioration Of The Mind

Romans 1:21-22 reveals a natural progression leading from vanity to deterioration of the mind: *"Because that, when they knew God, they glorified him not as God, neither were thankful; but became vain in their imaginations, and their foolish heart was darkened. 22 - Professing themselves to be wise, they became fools."* A darkened heart means a darkened subconscious mind. The word **darkened** in the Bible is usually associated with the kingdom of Satan. It is also associated with depression. This First Chapter of Romans proceeds, in Verse 28, *"And even as they did not like to retain God in their knowledge, God gave them over to a reprobate mind, to do those things which are not convenient."* When one begins with vanity, things keep getting worse until he has a foolish heart, followed by a darkened heart, and finally a reprobate mind!

Does Pride Lead To Cancer?

Dr. Carl Simonton[2] is a therapeutic radiologist. With his wife, Stephanie, he statistically worked out the psychological profile of persons most prone to develop high grade malignancies. They discovered that the personality characteristics of such people included a history of parental rejection during childhood, a severe limitation in willingness

206

to forgive others, and a tendency to engage in self pity. E.M. Blumberg[1] conducted psychological tests on 50 patients who were diagnosed as having inoperable tumors. He discovered that patients with fast growing tumors characteristically had a greater than average motivation to appear good and less disturbed than they actually were, and a strong desire to conceal from others the fact that they were experiencing emotional problems.

An exaggerated tendency to conceal the fact that one has had or is having emotional problems is a manifestation of pride. To totally deny ever having emotional problems is to pretend to be a super-human being. This involves one's being dishonest both with himself and with others. Telling oneself that he does not have emotional problems when he is having such difficulty makes it unlikely that the problems will be improved or corrected. One is unlikely to change what he will not permit himself to see. The prideful person will not permit himself to see his own problems and conflicts, nor will he accept the counsel of anyone else.

I know that these studies are valid, because I had observed this personality type in people with highly malignant disorders before I knew that these studies existed. I have interviewed many people who had highly malignant illnesses. I have also spoken to many people whose relatives had such illnesses. The surviving relatives have often described these problematic personality characteristics of the deceased cancer victims. This is not to say that an overdeveloped self will or a great deal of pride is the only cause of malignant disease. There is merely a high correlation between having this type of personality and the development of highly malignant illnesses.

Characteristics of Masochism

The term **masochism** refers to a subconscious tendency for one to get hurt by himself or by others. Such pain is often emotional, though it may be physical, social, vocational, or financial. This is an extremely common phenomenon. Masochism is a way of saying "No" to the good things which God wants to give to us. A person suffering from masochism may habitually treat people in such a manner that they are certain to respond to him with rejection or with a verbal attack. He may tend to quit just before he obtains important goals, such as graduation, job promotions, or raises. He may be a hypochondriac who gets the most mileage possible from any symptom of pain, illness, or depression. He may damage himself by choosing relationships with people who are certain to damage him repetitively because of their sadistic tendencies. He may repetitively destroy his financial stability by gambling. He may harm his life by means of alcohol, drug abuse, or tobacco. Masochism usually affects self image, because the person who tends to be masochistic usually has an inferiority complex: he uses his mind to repetitively place negative labels upon himself, downgrade his abilities or self worth, or to chastize himself with self degrading suggestions around the clock. He chronically feels that he will not be able to do the things which the Lord wants him to do. He tends to always expect the worst, and therefore experiences the worrying habit. The masochistic person mentally devalues whatever God gives to him, i.e., position, skills, work, material provisions, relationships, and the protection which God provides. The Bible does not recommend masochism, and it has no proper place in healthy, effective Christian life.

Humility

Humility is the attitude which the Scriptures recommend. It is the position of stability between pride and masochism, and is generally misunderstood. People frequently confuse humility with being masochistic. For example, one normally thinks of a humble person as someone with a very low self image, who doesn't think much of himself or of his abilities. That is not what the Scriptures mean by humility. By

208

humility, the Bible means having a humble attitude toward God. A humble attitude toward God actually produces a very good self image, because a person with such an attitude feels that he can do anything that God wants him to do or gives him to do. A person who is humble toward God feels that he can face any situation. This is quite different from the average person's concept of being humble.

Everyone Is Humbled By Sin

One of the things that has impressed me in learning about the personal lives of a large number of people in my psychiatric practice is that it appears that everyone has experienced or done something of which he is ashamed. If our personal lives were flashed upon a screen before a large audience, most of us would be deeply ashamed, In my experience, the people who wouldn't be ashamed do not see their lives as objective observers would see them. For example, many people feel that they were good parents, but they lack adequate mercy, or empathy to realize the emotional damage which they inflicted upon their children by not giving them adequate time, attention, respect, or love during their childhood years. We have all done things which we prefer that no one know about. This has been the case with every life I have come to know. Because of the obvious prevalence of this in my observation, I began to wonder, "What is this all about? Why does everyone seem to have something in his life of which he would be ashamed if others knew about it?" It is rather common for people to tell their psychiatrists something that they would not even want their own spouses to ever know. It is not even unusual for people to conceal important secrets from their psychiatrists. That's how embarassing past sins can be!

The Bible confirms this concept. Romans 3:10 teaches, *"As it is written, There is none righteous, no, not one."* Romans 3:23 says, *"For all have sinned, and come short of the glory of God."* In 1 John 1:8, the Bible tells us, *"If we*

209

say that we have no sin, we deceive ourselves, and the truth is not in us." That is a very simple statement, and yet extremely important. If we feel that we have no sin, we are actually victims of self deception, which is the destructive component of pride. When we get carried away with pride, we do not see ourselves the way another person would see us, or the way God sees us. John gets even more pointed. In 1 John 1:10, he writes, *"If we say that we have not sinned, we make him (God) a liar, and his word is not in us."* I do not see how one can get more emphatic than that. If anyone feels that he is without sin, he is unwittingly attempting to make a liar of God, for God said that all have sinned, and even sent His Son to die because of this. No one is proud of anything that would be labeled a sin once he becomes able to see his life as God sees it.

God Calls The Humble And Humbles The Called

One thing that has become apparent to me as I have addressed this subject through the Scriptures, is that God calls the humble, and He humbles the called. In 1 Corinthians 1:26-29, Paul writes, *"For ye see your calling, brethren, how that not many wise men after the flesh, not many mighty, not many noble, are called. 27 - But God hath chosen the foolish things of the world to confound the wise; and God hath chosen the weak things of the world to confound the things which are mighty; 28 - And base things of the world, and things which are despised, hath God chosen, yea, and things which are not, to bring to nought things that are: 29 - That no flesh should glory in his presence."* This is a clear statement that God wants humble people to do His work. It is not likely to be someone who is extremely wealthy, or extremely wise in the ways of the world. It is not likely to be someone who has great political power, or an extremely high intelligence. It may happen that way, but it is unlikely. As a matter of fact, God would even prefer to call someone base, who has been somehow disgraced, than to call someone who is wise, wealthy, or politically powerful. How come?

I think that one answer lies in 2 Corinthians 12:7-9 as Paul writes, *"And lest I should be exalted above measure through the abundance of the revelations, there was given to me a thorn in the flesh, the messenger of Satan to buffet me, lest I should be exalted above measure. 8 - For this thing I besought the Lord thrice, that it might depart from me. 9 - And he said unto me, My grace is sufficient for thee: for my strength is made perfect in weakness."* Paul was given the thorn in the flesh so that he would not be exalted above measure and fall as Lucifer had done. In Galatians 4:13-14 Paul reveals more about his affliction (Revised Standard Version): *"You know it was because of a bodily ailment that I preached the gospel to you at first; 14 - and though my condition was a trial to you, you did not scorn or despise me, but received me as an angel of God, as Christ Jesus."*

Paul doesn't say what his thorn in the flesh was. The fact that he didn't say what it was suggests that he may have been too embarrassed to name or describe it in his letter. Whatever it was, it was so embarassing that he is thanking the Galatians for not having scorned him, and for not having despised him. He obviously **expected** to be scorned and despised by observers of his physical condition. He may have had a dreaded skin disease that severely marred his appearance. Whatever it was, whoever observed Paul would know that he was afflicted. No one would thank people for not despising his appearance unless something was obviously awful about it.

We can see that God humbled Paul by letting him have this thorn in the flesh. Many miracles were performed through Paul. It would have been very easy for him to get carried away with himself through pride. The Book of Acts, in Chapter 14, describes how Paul healed the man at Lystra who had never walked from birth. The people who saw this began to shout (V. 11), *"The gods are come down to us in the likeness of men."* Paul and Barnabas rejected this attempt of the crowd to make false gods of them. Instead, they preached the deity of Christ. How easy it would have been for a man who had not been humbled to permit the crowds to worship him! That would have been the end of Paul's Christian ministry. Yet, this was only one of many miracles performed through him.

Paul had yet another thorn in his life, something else of which to be ashamed. He had persecuted all of those Christians prior to his conversion. Some awful things happened to those people whom he had apprehended. The Scriptures teach us that God calls people for salvation (1 Corinthians 1:9, Titus 3:5). Christ Himself made a personal appearance to Paul on the road to Damascus, and converted him (Acts, Chapter 9). Christ could have chosen any point in Paul's life to convert him and call him to his Christian ministry. But Christ waited until Paul did all those awful things to so many Christians. As a result of that, Paul had to look back on what he had done when he had been doing things his own way. He had to look back upon every one of those Chirstians whose lives he damaged or destroyed. This was a very humbling experience. Paul writes in 1 Corinthians 15:9-10, *"For I am the least of the apostles, that am not meet to be called an apostle, because I persecuted the church of God. 10 - But by the grace of God I am what I am: and his grace which was bestowed upon me was not in vain; but I laboured more abundantly than they all: yet not I, but the grace of God which was with me."* We thus see that Paul was quite humbled by his past sins, and this apparently resulted in his working more abundantly than all of the other apostles. This spiritual thorn may have been even worse than the physical thorn. This pattern of painful past sins is very prevalent among the great prophets in the Bible.

Moses murdered an Egyptian at age forty, and was called by God at age eighty to lead Israel out of Egypt. God could have called anyone, but He went all the way to the "back side of a desert" and called a fellow who had been guilty of a murder. When God told Moses that he was to go into Egypt and lead the Jews out, Moses replied that he couldn't do that, because he had difficulty with speech. At that point, Moses went from humility to masochism. A person is being masochistic when he says to God, "No, I can't do what you have given me to do. I'm not good enough." The Bible tells us that God got angry with Moses for doing that. God responded by letting Aaron do the speaking for Moses. Imagine how easy it would have been for Moses to get carried away with himself and to become an egomaniac when he saw all the miracles that God provided through him! But the Bible says that Moses was the humblest man on earth (Numbers 12:3).

In Acts, Chapter 4, Verse 13, the Bible tells us, *"Now when they saw the boldness of Peter and John, and perceived that they were unlearned and ignorant men, they marveled; and they took knowledge of them, that they had been with Jesus."* Here is another example of two great men, Peter and John, who were regarded as ignorant men by the masses because they apparently had never studied in a theological seminary or graduated from any university. Yet, here they were, teaching the crowds with their impressive knowledge of Christ. They were apparently humble men, who would have been considered low in social or educational class.

Conclusion

What is it that Christ wants us to be striving toward? As I have mentioned, pride results in saying "No" to the Lord because of self will dominating one's life in place of what God wants us to be doing. Mental masochism is another way of saying "No" to the Lord by saying, "Lord, I know you want me to do this or that, because of the Bible and the circumstances you have presented to my life; but I'm just so dumb, so bashful, I have such a low self image, I'm so anxious, and so depressed, that I couldn't possibly do that, you see." That's not what the Bible teaches us to do either. Neither pride nor masochism are recommended by the Bible.

The attitude recommended by the Bible is humility. Humility does not mean being self degrading. Rather, it

213

refers to being humble towards God. The humble person demonstrates the attitude, "Whatever God wants me to do is truly the best thing possible, and I will do it." There is no conflict, no anxiety, and no depression about it.

The Bible says many things about humility. In Psalms 25:9, we are told, *"The meek will he guide in judgment: and the meek will he teach his way."* Proverbs 22:4 teaches, *"By humility and the fear of the Lord are riches, and honour, and life."* In 1 Peter 5:3, Peter instructs the elders in the church, *"Neither as being lords over God's heritage, but being ensamples to the flock."* This can be applied to each of us. We shouldn't act like lords over whatever God gives us in terms of money, position, or anything else. We can simply portray effective examples of what others can become through Christ. In 1 Peter 5:5, the Bible teaches, *"Likewise, ye younger, submit yourselves unto the elder. Yea, all of you be subject one to another, and be clothed with humility: for God resisteth the proud, and giveth grace to the humble."*

The Scriptures point out that Christ set an example of humility which He expected us to follow. In John 13:13-17, Christ said, *"Ye call me Master and Lord: and ye say well; for so I am. 14 - If I then, your Lord and Master, have washed your feet; ye also ought to wash one another's feet. 15 - For I have given you an example, that ye should do as I have done to you. 16 - Verily, verily, I say unto you, The servant is not greater than his Lord; neither he that is sent greater than he that sent him. 17 - If ye know these things, happy are ye if ye do them."* What a promise! Christ demonstrated an attitude of humble service as the example to be followed. He concludes with a promise that those who know and do these things, i.e., follow His example, will be happy! This is a promise that must be fulfilled to whomever meets these conditions. Otherwise Christ would be made a liar, and He cannot lie. I know that this is true. The things that have made me happy have usually been things that involved serving other people, whether it be my children, my spouse, somebody else about whom I care, somebody who comes to me for help, or a stranger. These have been the things that have produced happiness in me. When I look at the lives of people who seem to be successful and at peace, they always turn out to be people who are primarily interested in somehow being of service. They feel good about themselves because of what they know they are doing for others. They know that their lives are valuable to other people, to God, and to themselves.

In Matthew 11:28-30, Christ teaches, *"Come unto me, all ye that labour and are heavy laden, and I will give you rest. 29 - Take my yoke upon you, and learn of me; for I am meek and lowly in heart: and ye shall find rest unto your souls. 30 - For my yoke is easy, and my burden is light."* Here is the Messiah Himself saying, "I am meek and lowly in heart." This simply means that He was humble in His relationship to God the Father. He could thus do anything that His Father wanted Him to do. One last Scripture regarding humility as Christ exemplified it is in John 6:37-38, where Christ says, *"All that the Father giveth me shall come to me: and him that cometh to me I will in no wise cast out. 38 - For I came down from heaven, not to do mine own will, but the will of him that sent me."* Here is a very clear statement by Christ Himself that He did not live by a prideful, self will. His only concern was that He do whatever His Father in heaven wanted Him to be doing. He thus set the example that we should follow, and gave us the solemn promise (John 13:17), *"If ye know these things, happy are ye if ye do them."*

Bibliography

[1]Blumberg, E.M. **Results of Psychological Testing of Cancer Patients.** In J.A. Gengerelli and F.J. Kirkner (eds.), **Psychological Variables In Human Cancer.** Berkeley and Los Angeles: University of California Press, 1954, pp. 30-61.

[2] Simonton, O. Carl and Stephanie S. **Belief Systems And Management Of The Emotional Aspects Of Malignancy. Journal of Transpersonal Psychology** 7:29-47, 1975.

13

Christian Methods Of Destroying Fear In Life Today

Fear! What is it all about, and how do you destroy it? A young man consulted a psychiatrist because he had destroyed his family unit with fear. He had become extremely suspicious of his wife, and had been continually accusing her of unfaithfulness, though he had no evidence of this whatsoever. He felt compelled to continually check on her whereabouts. After questioning her at length about where she had been, and with whom, he would make phone calls to check her stories. This had become such an obsession that she had decided that she could no longer live with him, and had left him. Their children were being hurt by the turmoil and the breakup. He wanted to overcome his obsession, because he had no hope of a reconciliation so long as he was acting like this.

A rapid analysis of his problem indicated that the subconscious reason he feared his wife would be unfaithful was that as a child, he had seen his father demonstrate a disastrous nervous breakdown in response to his mother's infidelity. He felt that if his wife were ever unfaithful, he too would have a nervous breakdown. He assumed that if he would continually question his wife about her whereabouts and conduct, she would realize that he would know it as soon as she were to be unfaithful. He reasoned that she would consequently not cheat on him. Unfortunately, his flawed plan of fearfulness had driven his wife away. He and she had been separated for months, and she wouldn't even speak with him about a reconciliation.

The problem was eliminated by his realizing why he had been compulsively accusing his wife, and that this was not a viable solution to his fear. It was suggested that he begin striving to become the spiritual leader of his family, and that he learn to claim the many promises in the Scriptures regarding God's protection and provision to those who follow Christ's teachings. This delivered him from his obsession, which was a bondage to fear. Here is a small glimpse of how destructive fear can be.

The Book of Revelation, in Chapter 21, Verses 7 and 8, gives us an important message about the subject of fear: *"He that overcometh shall inherit all things; and I will be his God, and he shall be my son. 8 - But the fearful, and unbelieving, and the abominable, and murderers, and whoremongers, and sorcerors, and idolaters, and all liars, shall have their part in the lake which burneth with fire and brimstone: which is the second death."* It is clear here, that in the eyes of God, being fearful can be as dreadful as being a murderer. This initially seems astounding. The average person will read that and think, "What kind of God could make such a statement, that He is going to cast the fearful into the lake of fire with the murderers and all those other categories of people? This becomes understandable when you consider what people will do out of fear. When David discovered that Bathsheba was pregnant with his child, it was the fear of his adultery with her being discovered that caused him to arrange the murder of her husband, Uriah. Initially, David lacked the faith which he later demonstrated, that God would see him through the consequences of his sins. This is how powerful fear can be when a man gives it dominion over him. David was a Godly, courageous man. Though he was of small build, he had willingly fought a battle to the death with the giant, Goliath, who was over nine feet tall. But when the time arrived to face and admit his sin, he gave fear dominion over him. This expensive experience of King David demonstrates that there is, in fact, a connection between fear and something as severe as murder. It was probably fear that God wouldn't properly handle the situation that caused Moses at age forty to murder that Egyptian soldier who was beating one of the Jews. That cost him forty years on the back side of the desert, to which he fled to escape Egyptian retribution.

Fear causes pain, suffering, disability, and actually causes many diseases. A young man was disabled by severe pain throughout his body. He felt that if he couldn't continually receive narcotic pain medication, he couldn't survive. A thorough evaluation of his condition revealed that he originally had a neuromuscular disease which had apparently subsided in the past. While the disease had been active, he had become addicted to the narcotic pain medication which he had been given. Since the physical disorder had subsided, his mind had been subconsciously generating pain in order to obtain regular doses of addicting drugs. As a tolerance would develop to each dosage level of the narcotics, his body would then generate higher levels of pain in order to obtain a larger dosage of the drugs. He had been seen by specialists in every field that was potentially related to his symptoms, and everyone felt that his condition was somehow emotionally caused.

A rapid analysis of his pain revealed that it was related to a fight during his teens, in which several other teenage boys had beaten him to the point of unconsciousness. Shortly before he was knocked out, he was hurting so badly that he felt that he couldn't take another lick. He had told himself at that moment, "If somebody hits me just one more time, I'm just going to die! I can't possibly survive another blow!" That thought stayed in his subconscious mind. From then on, that fear of getting hurt again revealed itself in the form of a fear of pain. That fear had destroyed the quality and goodness of his life. The moment that he experienced pain of any sort, he felt that he had to do **anything** necessary to immediately eliminate that pain. The outcome was his addiction to progressively increasing doses of narcotics.

Fear And Satanic Oppression

The Book of Hebrews has some very important things to say about the relationship between fear and satanic bondage in Chapter 2, Verses 14 and 15: *"Forasmuch then as the children are partakers of flesh and blood, he also himself took part of the same; that through death he might destroy him that had the power of death, that is, the devil; 15 - And deliver them who through fear of death were all their lifetime subject to bondage."* It is clear that fear is an important and common mechanism by which people place themselves in bondage to Satan. Fear is saying "Yes" to the devil. Fear is the opposite of faith, and therein lies its tremendous destructiveness. Faith is the courage to base your life on the fact that God will provide what is **needed** if you give him dominion of your situation (Philippians 4:19).

Psalms 34:7 contains the promise, *"The angel of the Lord encampeth round about them that fear him, and delivereth them."* Here the Bible is talking about fear of God. Fear of God is the exact opposite of all other types of fear. Fear of God means understanding that God is bound to fulfill every scriptural promise in our lives as the circumstances of our daily lives match the conditions given in the promises. When we see a Biblical promise like this one in Psalms, we know that God is bound to fulfill it once we place our lives under his dominion. We can thus claim this promise.

The Bible makes it clear that fear does not come from God. The Second Epistle of Paul to Timothy 1:7 teaches, *"For God hath not given us the spirit of fear; but of power and of love, and of a sound mind."* This makes it inevitable that fear must inevitably come from either human or Satanic origin.

The Scriptures give us emphatic authority over the power of Satan. James 4:7-8 promises, *"Submit yourselves therefore to God. Resist the devil, and he will flee from you.*

8 - Draw nigh to God, and he will draw nigh to you. " The Holy Spirit of God dwells in the spirits of Christians (1 Corinthians 3:16, 6:19, 2 Corinthians 13:5), and His power is ours to appropriate at will. The First Epistle of John 4:4 promises, *"Greater is he that is in you, than he that is in the world."* With such clear Biblical promises of authority over Satan, overcoming fear is clearly an available, personal choice. Phillipians 4:13 teaches, *"I can do all things through Christ which strengtheneth me."*

Early in my practice of psychiatry, I realized that fear is a major problem among the general population. The fearful person says to himself, "When I get enough courage, I'm going to actually drive my automobile. When I get enough courage, I am actually going to look for a job. When I get enough courage, I am going to take care of my children." Uncertainty, indecision, and conflict are hallmarks of fear. The fearful person wants to function, but is afraid to do so. He may demonstrate the condition referred to in James 1:5-8 as **double-minded:** *"If any of you lack wisdom, let him ask of God, that giveth to all men liberally, and upbraideth not; and it shall be given him. 6 - But let him ask in faith, nothing wavering. For he that wavereth is like a wave of the sea driven with the wind and tossed. 7 - For let not that man think that he shall receive any thing of the Lord. 8 - A double minded man is unstable in all his ways."* In my first reading of the Bible years ago, I was impressed with the large number of Scripture verses in both Old and New Testaments in which God commands or admonishes us through His prophets to fear not, and to have courage. Examples of these are Deuteronomy 31:6, 8, and 23; Zechariah 8:13, John 14:27. God not only commands us to have courage, but He is obviously quite disappointed in anyone who is fearful.

The thought occurred to me that God would not command us to do anything unless we already had the ability to do it. Consequently, the ability to be courageous must already be in every human being. How can that be, with fear being such a common human experience? The answer is that courage begins as a **decision,** and then progresses to the level of **emotion.** If a person needs courage, he should not wait until he **feels** courage before beginning to **act** courageously. This is one of the most common mistakes of people who are suffering from fear and are overwhelmed by it. If a person who experiences anxiety or fear decides to act on the fear, he then demonstrates fear to himself and to those around him. Once he sees himself cringing with fear, retreating from essential responsibilities, he then experiences an intensification of the **emotion** of fear. He then finds himself caught in an intensifying cycle of fear causing the demonstration of fear, which causes more fear, etc. But what happens when a person **refuses** to demonstrate fear? A person who finds himself in a stressful or dangerous situation may experience initial mild discomfort, anxiety, depression, or fear of the consequences. But he may mentally take hold of himself and say to himself, "No matter what the outcome of this situation, I am demonstrating courage that I and anyone who observes me will have to admire!" He can thus make the **decision** to demonstrate courage. This decision then begins rapidly destroying fear, anxiety, or depression. As the decision to demonstrate courage becomes firm and is put into action, the **emotion** of courage follows shortly behind. Fear is then destroyed.

I was once asked to teach techniques of pain control to a man who had been burned over half of his body. He was confined to a hospital room for many months, and exprienced all sorts of very severe problems. Yet, he was lying there inspiring everyone who went into his room, because he was demonstrating courage. He could have demonstrated anything that he chose to demonstrate. He could have demonstrated fear, or agony, or depression, or despair. Instead, he decided that he was going to demonstrate courage, and that he did. He was completely disabled for a period of many months, even having to be fed, but he **could** do one thing: he could demonstrate courage.

Joni Eareckson is a quadraplegic woman who was

222

paralyzed from the neck down in a diving accident. After her injury, she became an effective artist by painting with the brush in her mouth. She has written several inspiring books and has given her testimony on the Billy Graham Crusade. During her testimony, she demonstrated an inspiring courage. She could have demonstrated fear, or self pity. Instead, she chose to demonstrate courage, and became a source of inspiration to millions of people.

The Bible Promises Us Dominion Over Fear And Its Causes: Will We Accept It?

The 91st Psalm has a lot to say about fear, terror, and the devil. Here God promises something about all those things. *"He that dwelleth in the secret place of the most High shall abide under the shadow of the Almighty. 2 - I will say of the Lord, He is my refuge and my fortress: My God; in him will I trust."* Here the Bible is saying that if you will place yourself under the dominion of God, He promises to protect you. In Verse 3, the Bible continues, *"Surely he shall deliver thee from the snare of the fowler, and from the noisome pestilence."* A pestilence is an epidemic of infectious disease. He will deliver you from disease, and from traps.

In Verse 4 the promises continue, *"He shall cover thee with his feathers, and under his wings shalt thou trust: his truth shall be thy shield and buckler. 5 - Thou shalt not be afraid for the terror by night; nor for the arrow that flieth by day; 6 - Nor for the pestilence that walketh in darkness; nor for the destruction that wasteth at noonday. 7 - A thousand shall fall at thy side, and ten thousand at thy right hand; but it shall not come nigh thee. 8 - Only with thine eyes shalt thou behold and see the reward of the wicked. 9 - Because thou hast made the Lord, which is my refuge, even the Most High, thy habitation; 10 - There shall no evil befall thee, neither shall any plague come nigh thy dwelling. 11 - For he shall give his angels charge over thee, to keep thee in all thy ways. 12 - They shall bear thee up in their hands, lest thou dash thy foot against a stone. 13 - Thou shalt tread upon the lion and adder: the young lion and the dragon shalt thou trample underfeet. 14 - Because he hath set his love upon me, therefore will I deliver him: I will set him on high, because he hath known my name. 15 - He shall call upon me, and I will answer him: I will be with him in trouble; I will deliver him, and honour him. 16 - With long life will I satisfy him, and shew him my salvation."*

It is difficult to imagine any source of fear that is not covered by this 91st Psalm. God clearly promises His protection to anyone who will place himself and his situation under God's dominion and protection. The average person who reads this Psalm tends to think, "It's great that prophets had such a personal relationship with God thousands of years ago. I wish such a relationship were available to me today."

In 1978, I heard the testimony of a Methodist missionary who had recently escaped from the country of Zaire during the bloody rebellion there, in which many people were slaughtered. He and his wife and children were in a house when they saw an approaching band of rebel soldiers who had been slaughtering both blacks and whites in that area. He and his family knelt in the house and prayed. They claimed God's promises in the 91st Psalm. They verbally placed themselves under God's protection and asked God to blind the soldiers to the missionary's house, so that whenever they looked toward the house, they would see only an open field. The Rebels camped fifty yards from the house, and never entered it!

In Philippians 4:4-7, Paul writes, *"Rejoice in the Lord alway: and again I say, Rejoice. 5 - Let your moderation be known unto all men. The Lord is at hand. 6 - Be careful for nothing; but in everything by prayer and supplication with thanksgiving let your requests be made known unto God. 7 - And the peace of God, which passeth all understanding, shall keep your hearts and minds through Christ Jesus."*
Important spiritual and emotional lessons are given here. The Revised Standard Version translates Verse 6 as, *"Have no*

224

anxiety about anything. ...." A combination of prayer, supplication, and thanksgiving will destroy fear, destroy anxiety, destroy worry. How? Whenever a stressful, threatening, or dangerous situation faces us we can react by prayer in which we share our concerns and needs with the Lord and ask Him to provide what He knows that we need. In supplication, we can humble ourselves before the Lord and acknowledge that He is infinitely wiser than we are, and that whatever He provides in any situation is truly the best thing for our lives. In thanksgiving, we can thank God for whatever He has done, is doing, and will do in our lives, based on His infinite love, wisdom, and power. This type of praying is extremely effective in destroying fear, anxiety, and worry. It is probably the type of praying with which Paul courageously built and maintained the most successful ministry in the history of the Christian Church, throughout multiple beatings and imprisonments in dungeons. Here in Philippians, Paul teaches that the end result of prayer, supplication, and thanksgiving is peace.

Historically, Paul wrote the Epistle to the Philippians while he was in prison, probably at Rome. If Paul could destroy fear and find the peace of God while imprisoned in a dungeon, you and I can do likewise in spite of our tribulations! Here in Philippians, Paul presents the method: a personal, prayerful, humble, thankful relationship with Jesus Christ.

14

Properly Attuning The Conscience For Effective, Healthy, Christian Living

The conscience is an extremely important aspect of the individual's relationship with himself. One's conscience is like a violin. If the violin's strings are tuned too loosely, the instrument produces sounds which are too low in pitch and are out of tune with the rest of the orchestra. If the strings are tuned too tightly, the violin is again out of tune, producing pitches which are higher than the rest of the orchestra. Either way, the instrument will produce discord. Similarly, if one's conscience is too lose, or defective, it will produce discord in his emotional, spiritual, and behavioral life. If one's conscience is over-developed and punitive, it will again produce discord in every dimension of his existence. A properly attuned conscience is necessary for effective, healthy Christian life to be conducted on the spiritual, emotional, and behavioral levels. The foundation of a properly attuned conscience is that the individual's values agree with everything that Christ said regarding sin as well as Christ's teachings regarding His love and His forgiveness.

Conditions Of Inadequate Or Defective Conscience Produce Disaster

It is unfortunately common that individuals run their lives with consciences that are inadequate, non-developed, or damaged and defective in some way. The most blatant form of defective conscience is seen in the individual who has what is referred to as a **sociopathic personality**, or an **anti-social personality**. These labels refer to individuals who engage in activities in the criminal realm, or other activities which damage other people as well as themselves, with little or no concern about the consequences. Individuals with sociopathic or anti-social personalities are often imprisoned because of convictions of crimes.

A second category of defective conscience consists of what has been referred to as **superego lacunae**[1] or isolated defects of conscience. The Bible teaches the concepts of a **wounded** conscience and a weak conscience in 1 Corinthians 8:12, *"But when ye sin so against the brethren, and wound their weak conscience, ye sin against Christ."* It is more common for the conscience to be damaged, or defective, than absent. One of the more common examples of a wounded conscience is seen in the everyday acts of adultery which are so prevalent in society. It is extremely common for people who commit either adultery or fornication to tell themselves that somehow scriptural teachings regarding these acts do not apply to them. In Proverbs 30:20, Solomon gives us a very important lesson through the inspiration of the Holy Spirit on this subject: *"Such is the way of an adulterous woman; she eateth, and wipeth her mouth, and saith, I have done no wickedness."* Likewise, individuals who are alcoholics tend to justify their behavior by saying that they are not hurting anyone, and that they are really not alcoholics: they only get drunk on weekends rather than every day. The thief tells himself that he is not doing wrong, because he steals from people who are rich, or who abuse the poor. Such methods of rationalizing are common in all forms of sin.

There is a peculiar relationship between sin and wounding of the conscience. Let us say that an individual's conscience is urging him not to commit a particular act that he has not commited before, such as adultery, or theft, or whatever. He nonethless overrides his conscience with his will, and commits

227

the act anyway. Each time that he overrides his conscience, he is likely to damage it and gradually extinguish the conscience for that category of behavior. This is especially true if the individual is committing an act which is momentarily very pleasurable, such as certain sexual acts. It has been found by practitioners of behavior therapy, that one way to overcome anxiety is through pleasure. For example, individuals who experience various forms of sexual dysfunction characterized by high levels of anxiety regarding sex, have been treated by some therapists by gradually, progressively associating pleasurable physical sensations with contact with a member of the opposite sex. The pleasure gradually overrides the anxiety and extinguishes it.

An alcoholic individual likewise may use pleasure to suppress and extinguish his conscience. Whenever he is drunk, he may engage in behavior that he finds very pleasurable, such as brawling, beating his castrating wife, or uttering very profane and hostile words to family members who have offended him. The alcohol has removed his usual inhibitions. Relieving chronic pent-up hostility toward parents and spouse, which has been causing depression, thus produces pleasure which diminishes or wounds the conscience regarding this type of behavior. Each time that he engages in such behavior and enjoys it, it is easier to do it next time.

A person who engages in theft may receive pleasure from several sources. He may be suffering from chronic bitterness towards parents. He may subconsciously wish to retaliate against them by embarrassing and disappointing them by his ultimate arrest. Inflicting loss on the people from whom he steals may permit him to feel subconsciously that he is retaliating against parents by mentally transferring the bitterness toward parents to his victims. Also, monetary pleasure may be derived from money or other items that he steals when he spends or uses them. The pleasure likewise suppresses or wounds his conscience regarding the stealing behavior. Each theft makes the next one a bit easier, because the conscience responds with less intensity. A Christian conversion experience may restore a wounded conscience to health by the Holy Spirit's convicting one in order to cleanse him and deliver him from his bondage to sin. Thus, the Bible's teaching of the wounded conscience is verifiable with the principles and practices of modern psychiatry and psychology.

In my clinical experience, even though a conscience may be consciously wounded and knocked out of function for the purpose of inhibiting a particular form of sinful behavior, the conscience will nontheless produce and generate subconscious guilt for that behavior. For example, it is not uncommon for women who obtain abortions or for men who pay for them to tell themselves that it was alright, and unavoidable; but many years later they are often still engaging in self damaging behavior as a result of subconscious guilt about those acts. A woman may wound her conscience enough to feel that she was justified in aborting her fetus; but weeks, months, or years later, she may find herself prolonging, intensifying, or producing symptoms of a physical illness as a means of punishing herself for that abortion. She may maintain a chronic depression, chronic marital difficulties, or chronic financial problems as a result of subconscious guilt about that abortion. Each subconscious guilt may produce self contempt, which can cause one to isolate oneself from fellowship with God or other people because of feeling like too bad a person to have a relationship with God or anyone else.

A defective or wounded conscience may also result from identification with parental character defects. A child uses his parents as models for his own behavior. Gradually, the child reaches an adequate level of intellectual maturity to realize that his parents are demonstrating character defects in the troubled areas of their lives. He is able to see that those character defects are the opposite of the character of Christ, which the Bible instructs us to reproduce in our own lives. So long as a child avoids bitterness, he may see the character of Christ through his parents' character defects, and may produce a healthy identification with Christ's character in those areas. Unfortunately, if a child was hurt by his parents' character defects, he may have become embittered toward the parents for their rejection or abuse of him. The bitterness intensifies his mental pre-occupation with his parents, which may cause him to identify with them more intensely than is normal. A rebellious attitude is a common response to chronic bitterness toward parents because of their character defects. One may rebel against God, rebel against parental values, and become a **liberated** person, or rebellious spirit. He may consequently feel a compulsion to be a drunkard, or a thief, or an adulterer, or a verbally abusive or violent person, like his hated parents. His only hope for freeing himself from the dominion of his hatred and negative identification is to decide to forgive his parents. Forgiveness can be rendered for his own good, and will free him from the pain of the past.

Conditions of Exaggerated Or Punitive Conscience

Just as a defective or wounded conscience can produce havoc in one's life, so can an exaggerated conscience. In this condition, the conscience becomes something other than what God intended for it to be. A severely over-developed conscience can severely inhibit or wreck an individual's effectiveness. He may become afraid to do any normal thing, for fear that he may make an error, or offend someone, or function less than perfectly. He may be fearful that his own feelings of self contempt will be shared by other people who observe him in action. Such a person projects his self contempt or self hatred, attributing to others his hateful attitude toward himself. He expects others to criticize him. An individual with an over-developed conscience inevitably experiences self contempt, or self hate. This results in depression and despair, and is in contradiction to Christ's teachings in Matthew 22:37-39. *"Thou shalt love the Lord thy God with all thy heart, and with all thy soul, and with all thy mind. 38 - This is the first and great commandment. 39 - And the second is like unto it, Thou shalt love thy neighbour as thyself.* "Here Christ puts loving yourself last, but He does include it. One must have a certain minimal amount of respect for oneself as a child of God who can be used as an instrument of the Lord. Without this self respect, one is unable to respect or love anyone else. This is not to be confused with pride or conceit. One can be humble toward God and yet acknowledge the fact that God loves him, and that he is the child of a king.

The individual with an exaggerated or punitive conscience misuses his conscience to damage himself by frequent, derogatory remarks uttered silently to himself. This often results from over-critical parents who directed a barrage of criticisms to the individual throughout childhood. The individual simply identified with the harsh, overcritical attitudes of his parents toward him. In adult life, his thoughts about himself are reproductions of his parents' hostile statements to him. Another contributing cause of such a punitive conscience is hatred of parents who maintained such a destructive attitude toward one in childhood. Hatred of a parent combined with identification with that parent produces self hatred. Such self hatred, or self contempt is often the cause of chronic, degrading thoughts about oneself, as well as an unforgiving attitude about oneself.

An exaggerated or punitive conscience often produces combinations of masochistic and sadomasochistic disorders. Such disorders consist of chronic emotional and behavioral patterns of hurting both oneself and others. Examples of this are often seen in psychiatric practice in people who demonstrate obsessions with guilt. Such individuals may demonstrate hand washing compulsions. They chronically wash their hands all day in subconscious attempts to cleanse themselves of the guilt which they feel about past sins. These sins are often very minor in reality. Housewives obsessed with guilt will often leave the house a mess while they methodically worry about dirt and cleanliness. Parents who are obsessed

231

with guilt may engage in sloven child-rearing practices, because they feel too guilty to discipline their children. They may avoid sex with their spouse because, "It is dirty," and "Mother or father told me that sex was wrong." These are examples of individuals agreeing with their parents about a subject in direct contradiction to what God teaches us in the Scriptures. This inevitably produces damage to one's emotional health. The person who suffers from the guilt habit chronically uses guilt for the purpose of hurting and damaging himself. Instead, one should use guilt as a sign that he needs to correct some sinful behavior, and seek and accept God's forgiveness for that behavior.

The exaggerated or punitive conscience thus produces thought patterns which I call **mental garbage.** These thought patterns clutter the mind with rotten thoughts and rob their victims of mental and behavioral fruitfulness. In this condition of exaggerated or punitive conscience, the conscience, which is a very necessary and vital part of successful Christian living, may become one's own greatest enemy. This phenomenon is often satanic in its destructive effects upon one's mental health and effectiveness.

Characteristics Of A Healthy, Properly Attuned Conscience

In contrast to the previously mentioned conditions of underdeveloped or overdeveloped conscience, we come now to the phenomenon of a healthy conscience which is attuned with Christ's teachings and instructions. One important characteristic of a healthy conscience is that it agrees with God on sin. Those things which God has taught us in the Bible as sinful are acknowledged as wrong, inadvisable, and harmful. The person with a healthy conscience feels guilty if he engages in sinful behavior; however, the individual with a healthy conscience also agrees with God's promises of forgiveness as given in 1 John 1:9, *"If we confess our sins, he is faithful and just to forgive us our sins, and to cleanse us from all unrighteousness.''* The person with a healthy conscience also **accepts** this forgiveness which Christ promises, and accepts the blood of Christ as sufficient to atone for his sins (Romans 3:24-25, 5:12-21, Ephesians 1:7). The person with a healthy conscience will accept the abundant, parental love of Christ for His children even when they sin, just as human parents normally love their children even when **they** sin.

The person who has a properly attuned, healthy conscience does not merely concern himself with the fear that God will punish him if he disobeys God's laws. The healthy Christian brings into consideration God's love and wisdom. He realizes that the Bible's laws and teachings are important means by which God protects us from unforseen evil. He realizes that God's laws are also means by which God gives to us the best things possible for the fulfillment of His perfect plan for each of our lives.

Conclusion

The purpose of conscience is to prevent our engaging in sinful behavior as God defines it in the Bible, to encourage us to reverse our particular forms of recurrent, sinful behavior, and to help us to build character strengths in the areas of our character defects.

The development of a healthy conscience may be compared to the phenomenon of body weight. Eating proper amounts of a well balanced diet can produce ideal physical health, mental health, and body image. On the other hand, if one fails to eat, or eats very inadequately, he may become emaciated and begin suffering from a host of physical and mental derangements. The individual who grossly overeats may ruin his self image and self respect with obesity. He may also produce the physical disorders that may accompany obesity, such as hardening of the arteries, diabetes, respiratory difficulties, high blood pressure, and arthritis. Like body weight, the conscience must not be permitted to shrivel up or to overdevelop.

A healthy person rejects exaggeration as well as destruction of his conscience. The person with a healthy conscience uses his own past experience with sin and the sin tendency to become and remain humble toward God. This produces ever increasing character strengths and progressive spiritual and emotional growth and maturity. We can use past experience with our own sins to develop empathy for the sinful, human conditions of our neighbors, rather than nurturing a scornful, conceited attitude toward others. Conditions of either inadequate or over-developed conscience always represent some serious disagreements with what God has said about the sin tendency of the human condition, about sin, or about His grace and love for us. A healthy conscience produces a life that is intimately attuned with God's desire to protect us through His laws and instructions, with what He wants us to do, and with what He wants to give to us.

Bibliography

[1]Johnson, Adelaide, and Szurek, S.A. **The Genesis Of Anti-social Acting Out In Children And Adults. Psychoanalytic Quarterly**, 21:323-343, 1952.

15

The Truth Shall Make You Free From Anxiety, Fear, And Depression In Life Today

Sometime ago, I had the opportunity to see a young woman who claimed that she was being oppressed by a demon. Whenever she would utter one of her frequent psychotic statements, she would conclude it with, "The demon told me to say that." It was remarkable that each of these statements was an obvious spiritual lie. For example, she had previously publicly accepted Christ, and had been baptized. Yet, she would say things like, "He (the demon) says that my salvation wasn't real. I'm going to hell. Jesus doesn't love me." All of these things were obvious lies. Another such statement was, "He says that you're feeling contempt for me." I was not feeling any such thing.

I was very impressed with the lies that were coming out of her mouth each time that she prefaced her statements with, "He told me to say this." In John 8:44, Christ told the Pharisees that Satan is the father of lies, and there is no truth in him.

It was my impression that this woman was probably severely oppressed. Technically, it didn't make any difference in the initial stages of the therapy. She was so out of touch with reality that it was necessary that she be hospitalized and placed on antipsychotic medication. She was saying that this "thing" was telling her to kill herself. The Bible tells us in

235

John 10:10, *"The thief (Satan) cometh not, but for to steal, to kill, and to destroy."*

After several days in the hospital on medication, this "thing" was shut out, whatever it was. She became calm and rational. My next concern was that over the preceding several years, she had repetitively been on the borderline of psychosis during stressful situations. I was concerned with why this was happening to her.

After the psychotic verbalizations and thinking had subsided, she was able to describe several interesting things about her spiritual life. She apparently had the gift of discernment; she could sense evil spirits. She described past experiences of being in public places, such as sleazy restaurants, and suddenly feeling an awful, slimy feeling and sensing that she was in the presence of something evil. When she would look over at the individual who had just sat next to her, she could see that the individual's appearance was consistent with that of someone under the dominion of oppressing spirits. When she was no longer in the psychotic state, she told me that the day that this "nervous breakdown" occurred, she was at home in her bedroom and saw a shadowy black figure come into the doorway of her bedroom and leap at her. That was the beginning of the end of her mental health, until the time she was brought to me for treatment. One might say, "Well, this lady just became psychotic and was merely imagining all this." Yet, I don't think that is exactly what happened. I think that a combination of spiritual as well as emotional factors were at play in her illness.

My main concern was, "Why did all of this happen to her?" Here was a born again Christian who said that she was being affliced by a demon, and she had literally lost her mind. I wanted to know why! My previous experience had indicated to me that individuals who experience this type of thing have been previously maintaining some areas of their lives unconsecrated to Christ. People may make a decision for Christ in one day and become Christians, but it subsequently takes a long period of time for them to methodically go through their lives and consecrate each area of their lives to Christ. I told her that I was concerned with what it was that had opened her life up to such an un-Godly experience. I asked her to go home and make a list of all those things that existed in her life and that had not yet been consecrated to the Lord.

The next week she returned to my office and said, "I tore the list up. It was so long, I got discouraged! I've been bitter because my last child confined me to the house, bitter about where I live, and bitter about my neighbors. I've been bitter about my church, bitter that the members don't accept me, bitter about my husband's work, and about his church activities." As I listened to the theme of what she was saying, it was apparent that she had a very negative attitude about everything. The common denominator of her complaints seemed to be that she had the habit of engaging in self pity. Once that self pity would occur, every life experience, good or bad, became an excuse for despair. Once she began despairing, she was open for any type of emotional and spiritual evil. She would even despair about the fact that God had given her a beautiful, healthy child.

I began pointing out to her that she had placed herself under the dominion of lies. Lie Number One was, "What God wants to give me is not the best that I could have." This is the same lie that Satan presented to Eve in Eden: if she and Adam would just eat of that Tree of Knowledge of Good and Evil and disobey God, they would somehow have something better than what God wanted them to have. Now we know, of course, that this was quite untrue. This is the lie behind all lies. Whenever I am trying to understand any emotional illness, I can always identify at least one, and usually several lies which caused the onset of the illness. Once a person gives a lie dominion over his mind, a pattern begins in which lies beget lies, which beget more lies.

Three important concepts will be discussed in this presentation. First, there is a lie behind every emotional illness. Second, recognizing that lie, rejecting it, and replacing it with truth frees one from the bondage of that emotional illness. Third, all truth gets back to God.

Lies Cause Anxiety and Depression

We could go through all of the various things that emotionally afflict people, and identify the lies behind them. I'll touch on many of those things here. The most common emotional disorder is depression. Depression is always caused by either bitterness toward God, bitterness toward one's fellow man, or bitterness toward oneself. The bitterness toward God always results from the lie mentioned above: that what God has given me is not the best thing for me. Bitterness toward one's fellow man is always based on the lie, "It is better to hold on to bitterness than to exercise forgiveness." The lies behind bitterness toward oneself are, "It is better to hold on to this self contempt than to accept Christ's atonement and His forgiveness. It is better to hate myself than to accept Christ's love for me." Another lie behind self contempt is that it is a rejection of Christ's teachings that we can reproduce His character in our lives, in spite of our past sins. The truth is that He can make our lives something beautiful, regardless of what we may have done with and to our lives in the past.

All forms of anxiety have some lie behind them. When we look at the causes of anxiety, we discover the functioning of the subconscious mind. The subconscious mind is by definition an enormous lie, because it represents the phenomenon of a mind directing our lives totally outside of our awareness, with totally different motivations from what we say to ourselves that our real motivations are. Our lives are thus being run by lies to ourselves and to others, so long as we are running our lives by our subconscious minds.

In **Outsmarting The Subconscious Mind By Christ Directed Living In Life Today,** I pointed out that it is not necessary to despair about the fact that we have subconscious minds that would ruin our lives. Through Christ directed living, we can short-circuit the subconscious mind so that we are doing what Christ wants us to do, thinking what Christ wants us to think, and feeling what Christ teaches us to feel in response to situations, rather than what the subconscious mind would have us do.

The Subconscious Mind's Mechanisms Of Defense Against Anxiety Are Lies

The subconscious mind demonstrates the phenomenon of **denial,** in which we deny to ourselves the truth of our real feelings about matters, to the point that those feelings become totally repressed outside of our awareness. The subconscious utilizes **projection,** a phenomenon in which we mentally project our own feelings onto other people and attribute our feelings to them. This is the cause of paranoid thinking. The paranoid person disowns his hostile wishes toward others and then believes that they feel that way about him. The subconscious phenomenon of **introjection** occurs when our bitterness toward other people becomes turned in upon ourselves. When that happens, we experience depression. The depressed person usually denies to himself that he is bitter toward anyone. He thus lies to himself and is unable to realize the cause of his depression until he gets honest with himself, faces and acknowledges his own anger. Through the subconscious, feelings can get converted into physical symptoms. A person may experience paralysis, or a peptic ulcer, or a severe pain syndrome, as a result of the subconscious mind converting feelings into physical phenomena. The lie there becomes, "There is nothing troubling me emotionally, it is only some physical problem."

There is a lie behind every psychosis. Interviewing someone who is psychotic usually reveals that much of what he says consists of obvious lies, though it is apparent that he is believing it. Schizophrenic psychotic thinking is an unsuccessful defense against anxiety, and is considered by many to consist of the following lies. At a critically early age, the individual feels that his parents are hurting him very badly or rejecting him. He feels so angry that he would like to kill the parents. Yet, he feels at some level that if he were to annihilate his parents, he would not survive. He is thus in severe conflict. He mentally attempts to get out of his emotional bind by the following distorted reasoning: "I don't really want to kill my parents. I'm not even angry with my parents. I'm not even the person who experienced all of that hurt and rage. I'm somebody else. As a matter of fact, my parents aren't even real; for that matter, neither am I." From that point, the emotional and mental confusion escalates without limit. A hospitalized, schizophrenic person recently said to me, "I am upset by the death of my mother. But she's not dead. I can change things by thinking about them. As a matter of fact, I'm not even here in this hospital. The person in this bed is not even I, because I'm somewhere else."

The alcoholism and drug addition cases that I have seen have always been associated with severely troubled relationships with God. These people had very bad childhood relationships with their earthly fathers, upon whom they could never depend in crises. They had consequently become very distrustful of God the Father. Whenever they faced any crisis in life, they felt that rather than depend upon God, they would rather count on the alcohol, or count on the barbiturates, or count on the heroin, or count on the pain pills that some doctor had prescribed for their pain syndromes, which were really part of their drug addition problems. The lie in addiction is, "God the Father is unreliable, because he must be like my unreliable, or weak, or rejecting, or abusive, earthly father."

Many individuals have felt that they were unable to face some loss which they sustained. It may have been a severe financial loss, or the loss of a child, or a spouse, or a parent, or a limb, or the loss of some bodily function. Such people may experience severe emotional illness as a result of their assumed inability to sustain their losses. One can often see spiritual and emotional lies such as the following in these situations. "What I have lost is more important to me than my relationship with God. God either doesn't know my needs, or doesn't care about me, or He lacks the power to help me. What God wants for me is not the best that I could have. I am such a weak, helpless child, that I cannot possibly face this stressful loss."

Biblical Examples Of Lives Damaged By Lies

There are many Biblical examples of lives which were ruined by lies. I've mentioned Adam and Eve. The life of Samson illustrates the ruination of a life through lies. God gave Samson the judgeship over Israel, and gave him incredible physical power. Yet, Samson's behavior demonstrated the following attitudes. "I've got to have evil women in my life in order to make it. What God wants me to have is not alright. I've got to visit prostitutes, and I've got to be intimate with Delilah, the Philistine, even though God has prohibited it." We know what happened. He was destroyed by Delilah and the Philistines as a result of rejecting what God wanted to give him. He engaged in un-Godly, inadvisabe forms of behavior which finally produced his undoing.

Something very similar happened to David in his relationship with Bathsheba, and in his subsequent spiritual error of conducting a census of Israel and Judah to determine how great a king he was. Yet, David illustrated the willingness and ability to get back under the protection of what God wanted to give him. He repented, and accepted whatever punishments God provided, though some of them were dreadful. He saw his way through them, and when the situational storms in his life were over, his life was okay again. He was subsequently admired as one of the greatest kings in the history of the Jews.

You can see the role of lies in the life of King Nebuchadnezzar. He took the position that all of the tremendous glory of Babylon was for him. The Bible tells us that God responded by permitting him to become a raging maniac, living like an animal in the fields for seven years. It is very interesting that in Daniel 4:34-37, the Bible says that Nebuchadnezzar's reason returned to him at the same time (v. 36), that he lifted his eyes toward heaven and praised God and acknowledged God's everlasting dominion over all generations. It apparently took seven years of living out in the fields like an animal before he would recognize and correct the lie of conceit and recognize that God's sovereignty was greater than that of Nebuchadnezzar's or of any false god.

King Asa was a very Godly man, but 2 Chronicles Chapter 16 describes how he got into difficulty in his relationship with the Lord when he developed a bitter attitude toward God. He developed a disease of his feet, and refused to turn to the Lord for healing. His attitude reflected the lie, "I don't need God. I'll just turn to my physician instead." Some people read that and say, "Well, that's the reason why you should never see physicians, but rather only pray." Many people do believe that if one goes to physicians, he is being un-Christian, and that he can't then expect God to heal him. That is not really the spiritual truth here. The Bible is teaching that we must recognize God's sovereignty in all healing, whether it is done through a physician, through prayer, or some other way. Luke was a physician, and Christ said in Matthew 9:12, *"They that be whole need not a physician, but they that are sick."* Some Bible historians also speculate that King Asa's physicans were actualy sorcerors. King Asa died of his disease, because he refused to turn to God.

Truth Heals The Mind

While the Bible occassionally uses the word **soul** in reference to the spirit, it seems that most of the Bible's uses of the word **soul** are obvious truths about the mind. In 1 Peter, Chapter 1, Verse 22, the Bible says, *"Seeing ye have purified your souls in obeying the truth through the Spirit unto* unfeigned love of the brethren, see that ye love one another with a pure heart fervently.'' It is a psychological truth that unfeigned Christian love of others will cleanse or purify one's mind of bitterness and depression. It is also a spiritual truth that love is better than bitterness or hatred.

In 2 Corinthians, Chapter 10, Verses 3 to 5, Paul writes, *"For though we walk in the flesh, we do not war after the flesh: 4 - (For the weapons of our warfare are not carnal, but mighty through God to the pulling down of strong holds;) 5 - Casting down imaginations, and every high thing that exalteth itself against the knowledge of God, and bringing into captivity every thought to the obedience of Christ.''* Here Paul is writing about pulling down strongholds. When the Bible talks about pulling down strongholds, it is referring to strongholds of satanic influence. Health-destroying imaginations are cast down through obedience to Christ. At the beginning of this presentation, I described the plight of a woman who had lost her emotional health and was totally disabled mentally by psychotic imaginations which she felt were due to satanic influence. All of that had apparently been made possible by an attitude of self pity. In the common depressions caused by self pity, people are overlooking the spiritual truth that obedience to Christ will produce the best of health and the best of life.

In Psalms 40:11-12, David writes, *"Withhold not thy tender mercies from me, O Lord: let thy lovingkindness and thy truth continually preserve me. 12 - For innumerable evils have compassed me about: mine iniquities have taken hold upon me, so that I am not able to look up; they are more than the hairs of mine head; therefore my heart faileth me.''* Here David is saying basically that his sins are going to overcome him unless God will preserve him with His love and His truth.

Replacing Lies With Truth Heals Emotional Illness

In John Chapter 8, Verse 32, Christ teaches, *"And ye shall know the truth and the truth shall make you free.''* This is the basis for all analytic, Christian counselling.

A young alcoholic woman near the beginning of her adult life had nearly suicided several times during drunken binges. When she and I explored the cause of her being a drunkard, it turned out that she physically resembled her alcoholic father. Throughout her childhood, he had always told her, "You are exactly like me." That was a lie, but she believed it, she accepted it, and she lived it. She was demonstrating the result of living this lie by her own alcoholic behavior. A very common cause of emotional illness is the lie, "I am exactly like one of my parents who had severe emotional problems, or severe character defects." This woman refused to give up that lie and thereby rejected a healing.

A middle aged man had achieved a very high technological position with his company. He frequently had to fly internationally in order to fulfill the duties of his job. He sought help for a fear of flying which had begun several years previously, and which had become progressively worse with time. Because of this fear, he had been progressively avoiding assignments and asking that the company send others on assignments that demanded his position and skills. He had reached the point however, that this was becoming so commonplace that he felt that he was in jeopardy of either being fired or having to quit because of his severe anxiety about having to fly to the job assignments. The nature of his work demanded that he reach his designation by the most rapid means possible, which made flying unavoidable.

A rapid analysis of his problem revealed that as a child he had resided in a neighborhood in which it was necessary to be a member of a teenage gang in order to have some protection in the continual gang warfare in the area. The onset of his phobia several years previously had occurred during a very rough flight in which the flight attendant became visibly frightened in the presence of the passengers. At that moment, he became very afraid that he too would appear fearful to the other people present. It turned out that his greatest fear was not that the plane was in trouble, but that he would appear afraid to others. With each subsequent flight that he had to take thereafter, this fear that he would appear fearful to others became progressively worse, to the point that he sought to avoid flying.

It was pointed out to him in the analysis that fear of appearing afraid seemed to have been a repetition of the way he must have felt as a teenager in the gang activities. In that situation, all of the boys in a gang had to live in constant fear of annihilation from other gangs in the neighborhood. Yet, everyone lived according to an unspoken code of honor which demanded that no one ever acknowledge being afraid. When he was asked during the analysis if he would have been killed by his own gang had he ever demonstrated fear, he replied that he certainly would have been killed in such a situation. It was thus obvious that his fear of flying was really a fear of demonstrating fearfulness. That fear had begun in his teenage experiences with gang warfare. It was also pointed out to him during his analysis that he had a long track record of having faced large numbers of difficult, fearful situations, and that he had traditionally, consistently demonstrated courage to others in these situations, no matter what he felt inside. He thus had no worry whatsoever of demonstrating fearfulness, because this was simply not a part of his personality and character structure.

He had thus reached the verge of complete, vocational incapacitation through this phobia of flying, all because of the simple subconscious lie, "If I demonstrate fear, I will be killed." When this lie in his subconscious mind was revealed to him, rejected, and replaced with the truth, he was dramatically, instantly healed. The truth, of course, was first of all, he would not be killed if he demonstrated fear, and second, he had already proven through many life experiences that he was not a person who demonstrated fear, even in extremely fearful circumstances, even when he felt afraid.

His treatment took a total of two sessions. Thereafter, he was able to fly internationally with no discomfort whatsoever. He informed me that he was completely healed of his phobia of flying, and did not need any further treatment. This man's illness was a clear illustration of the tremendous power of a lie to destroy one's mental health. It also clearly demonstrated the incredible power of truth to destroy his phobia, and dramatically free him from fear and anxiety.

What Is Truth?

The Bible associates truth with very important phenomena such as the following: truth and mercy (Psalms 25:10, 85:10, Proverbs 3:3); truth and kindness (2 Sam. 2:6); truth and sincerity (Joshua 24:14, 1 Corinthians 5:8); truth and righteousness (2 Chronicles 31:20); truth and peace (2 Kings 20:19, Isaiah 33:6); truth and meekness (Psalms 45:4); truth and love (Zechariah 8:19). Other things associated with truth are light (Psalms 43:3), goodness (Exodus 34:6, Ephesians 5:19), uprightness (Psalms 111:8), faithfulness (Isaiah 25:1), justice (Zechariah 8:16), soberness (Acts 26:25), grace (John 1:14), life (John 14:6), and spirit (John 4:23-24).

John 17:17 tells us that the word of God is truth: *"Santify them through thy truth: thy word is truth."*

Daniel 34:37 says that the works of God are truth. At the time that Nebuchadnezzar recovered from his seven year psychosis, he said, *"Now I Nebuchadnezzar, praise and extol and honor the King of Heaven, all whose works are truth and his ways judgment: and those that walk in pride he is able to abase."*

The First Epistle of John 5:6-7 tells us that the Holy Spirit is truth: *"And it is the Spirit that beareth witness, because the Spirit is truth. 7 - For there are three that bear record in Heaven, The Father, The Word, and The Holy Ghost. And these three are one."* In John, Chapter 16, Verse 13, Christ says, *"Howbeit when he, the Spirit of truth, is come, he will guide you into all truth."* Again, the Holy Spirit is referred to as truth.

Conclusion

In conclusion, there are one or several lies behind every emotional illness or distress. Recognizing each lie, rejecting it, and replacing it with truth, produces peace, joy, fruitfulness, and freedom from the bondage of that troubled emotion. All truth leads back to God. The Bible says that the works of God are truth, the word of God is truth, the Holy Spirit is truth, and Christ Himself said in John 14:6, *"I am the way, the truth, and the life."* He also said, in John 8:32, *"And ye shall know the truth, and the truth shall make you free."*